JESUS, HEAVEN ON EARTH

JESUS,
HEAVEN ON EARTH

Reflections on the Gospel for the A-Cycle

Joseph G. Donders

ORBIS BOOKS

Maryknoll, New York 10545

The Catholic Foreign Mission Society of America (Maryknoll) recruits and
trains people for overseas missionary service. Through Orbis Books Maryknoll
aims to foster the international dialogue that is essential to mission. The books
published, however, reflect the opinions of their authors and are not meant to
represent the official position of the society.

Library of Congress Cataloging in Publication Data

Donders, Joseph G
  Jesus, heaven on earth

Includes index.
  1. Bible. N. T. Gospels—Liturgical lessons,
English. I. Title.
BS2565.D66   266'.206   80-12602
ISBN 0-88344-241-8 (pbk.)

CONTENTS

INTRODUCTION   1

1. DOES HE DRUG US?   4
   (MATTHEW 24:37-44; FIRST SUNDAY OF ADVENT)

2. PRODUCING FRUITS   11
   (MATTHEW 3:1-12; SECOND SUNDAY OF ADVENT)

3. LIFE REGAINED   17
   (MATTHEW 11:2-11; THIRD SUNDAY OF ADVENT)

4. JESUS TO BE BORN   23
   (MATTHEW 1:18-25; FOURTH SUNDAY OF ADVENT)

5. JESUS, THE STRANGER   28
   (LUKE 2:1-14; CHRISTMAS)

6. MOST OF HIS TIME   34
   (MATTHEW 2:13-15, 19-23; FIRST SUNDAY AFTER CHRISTMAS)

7. A STAR AT ITS RISING   38
   (MATTHEW 2:1-12; THE EPIPHANY OF THE LORD)

8. A LAMB MISUNDERSTOOD   42
   (JOHN 1:29-34; SECOND SUNDAY)

9. THE NEW ALTERNATIVE   48
   (MATTHEW 4:12-23; THIRD SUNDAY)

10. HAPPINESS DID START   54
    (MATTHEW 5:1-12; FOURTH SUNDAY)

11. OF THE EARTH AND OF THE WORLD   60
    (MATTHEW 5:13-16; FIFTH SUNDAY)

12. THE OLD ENEMY   67
    (MATTHEW 4:1-11; FIRST SUNDAY OF LENT)

13. TO OPT UP AND OUT   74
(MATTHEW 17:1-9; SECOND SUNDAY OF LENT)

14. THE THIRST AT SAMARIA   79
(JOHN 4:5-42; THIRD SUNDAY OF LENT)

15. HE BEGAN TO SEE   87
(JOHN 9:1-41; FOURTH SUNDAY OF LENT)

16. DEAD AND BURIED   91
(JOHN 11:1-45; FIFTH SUNDAY OF LENT)

17. PITY TURNED ROUND   95
(MATTHEW 26:14-27:66; PASSION [PALM] SUNDAY)

18. THE EMPTY TOMB   99
(JOHN 20:1-9; EASTER SUNDAY)

19. THOMAS'S DOUBT   104
(JOHN 20:19-31; SECOND SUNDAY OF EASTER)

20. OUR OWN HOPE   108
(LUKE 24:13-35; THIRD SUNDAY OF EASTER)

21. HE IS THE OPEN DOOR   114
(JOHN 10:1-10; FOURTH SUNDAY OF EASTER)

22. TO TAKE YOU WITH ME   119
(JOHN 14:1-12; FIFTH SUNDAY OF EASTER)

23. JOHN'S SECRET CODE   126
(JOHN 14:15-21; SIXTH SUNDAY OF EASTER)

24. HE DID NOT STAY   133
(MATTHEW 28:19-20; ASCENSION DAY)

25. THE SPIRIT WE RECEIVED   140
(JOHN 20:19-23; PENTECOST)

26. OUR GOD   146
(JOHN 3:16-18; TRINITY SUNDAY)

27. SHARING ONE LOAF   149
(JOHN 6:51-58; CORPUS CHRISTI)

28. NOT THE SHOUTERS BUT THE DOERS   155
(MATTHEW 7:21-27; NINTH SUNDAY)

29. WORSHIP AND EXODUS 161
(MATTHEW 9:9-13; TENTH SUNDAY)

30. FIRST CAST OUT, THEN CURE 168
(MATTHEW 9:36-10:8; ELEVENTH SUNDAY)

31. IN THE PRESENCE OF PEOPLE 175
(MATTHEW 10:26-33; TWELFTH SUNDAY)

32. WE NEED A CHURCH 181
(JOHN 21:15-19; THIRTEENTH SUNDAY/PETER AND PAUL)

33. HIS BURDEN IS LIGHT 186
(MATTHEW 11:25-30; FOURTEENTH SUNDAY)

34. THE SEEDS OF THE KINGDOM 194
(MATTHEW 13:1-23; FIFTEENTH SUNDAY)

35. WHEAT AND WEED 200
(MATTHEW 13:24-43; SIXTEENTH SUNDAY)

36. THE KINGDOM IS HUMAN LIFE 205
(MATTHEW 13:44-52; SEVENTEENTH SUNDAY)

37. HE TOOK THEIR BREAD AND FISH 213
(MATTHEW 14:13-21; EIGHTEENTH SUNDAY)

38. HE STEPPED OUT OF HIS BOAT 220
(MATTHEW 14:22-33; NINETEENTH SUNDAY)

39. HE SAID NO 228
(MATTHEW 15:21-28; TWENTIETH SUNDAY)

40. THE ROCK UNDER THE KINGDOM 234
(MATTHEW 16:13-20; TWENTY-FIRST SUNDAY)

41. SAVING ONE'S LIFE 239
(MATTHEW 16:21-27; TWENTY-SECOND SUNDAY)

42. COMMUNITY DYNAMICS 244
(MATTHEW 18:15-20; TWENTY-THIRD SUNDAY)

43. RESTORATIVE POWER 248
(MATTHEW 18:21-35; TWENTY-FOURTH SUNDAY)

44. ROYAL SYNCHRONIZATION 252
(MATTHEW 20:1-16; TWENTY-FIFTH SUNDAY)

45. TO PRAY IS NOT ENOUGH   255
    (MATTHEW 21:28-32; TWENTY-SIXTH SUNDAY)

46. DELIVERING THE GOODS   259
    (MATTHEW 21:33-43; TWENTY-SEVENTH SUNDAY)

47. IT SHOULD BE A FEAST   264
    (MATTHEW 22:1-14; TWENTY-EIGHTH SUNDAY)

48. A TAX THAT IS NOT YET PAID   271
    (MATTHEW 22:15-21; TWENTY-NINTH SUNDAY)

49. WHY DOES OUR LOVE NOT WORK?   277
    (MATTHEW 22:34-40; THIRTIETH SUNDAY)

50. SOCIETY AS HE SAW IT   283
    (MATTHEW 23:1-12; THIRTY-FIRST SUNDAY)

51. A KINGDOM NOW   288
    (MATTHEW 25:1-13; THIRTY-SECOND SUNDAY)

52. LET US NOT BE AFRAID   293
    (MATTHEW 25:14-30; THIRTY-THIRD SUNDAY)

53. JESUS CHRIST KING   300
    (MATTHEW 25:31-46; LAST SUNDAY OF THE YEAR)

INDEX OF SCRIPTURAL TEXTS   307

INTRODUCTION

In Jesus
God
became
a human being.
　　Through him
　　heaven invaded
　　this world.
For Matthew
it was obvious
that in Jesus
humanity
came into
full being
too.
　　There was,
　　in a way,
　　no further need
　　to speculate
　　on God.
　　Theology was,
　　from the moment
　　of his birth,
　　about
　　our brother
　　Jesus Christ.
There was,
in a way,
no further need
to speculate
on human beings
either.

In Jesus
we human beings
were very concretely
confronted
with our own
fulfilment.
>To be confronted
>with him
>is no academic
>or esoteric
>exercise
>when it is done
>in the company
>of a student community
>in the heart of Africa.

The concreteness
of Jesus' life
is astonishingly
demanding
in the context
of the human authenticity
in Africa.
It is often painful
to the old way of life,
as well as inspiring.
>Matthew was convinced
>that Jesus was going
>to change the face
>of the earth.
>Going through his Gospel
>this conviction grew in us,
>at Saint Paul's in Nairobi,
>also.

To share this conviction
is the aim of this book,
which faithfully follows the
Gospel texts of liturgical year cycle A.

Because of that faithfulness
not all texts are from Matthew;
there are twelve from John
and two from Luke.
   Thy kingdom come,
   thy will be done,
   on earth
   as it is in heaven.

1.

DOES HE DRUG US?

Matthew 24:37-44

According to the authenticated reports
from Matthew, Mark, and Luke,
he said to his disciples
repeatedly:
"Stay awake,"
and
"Stand ready."
So it seems that,
according to him,
to fall asleep
or to be
asleep,
numbed,
unconscious,
unaware,
inattentive,
and drugged,
is the worst thing
we can do
in a world
in which we should live
and be awake.

4

When just before his arrest
his disciples
fell asleep again,
he reproached them
almost bitterly:
"Please,
can't you stay awake
with me
for one hour?"
And yet
when religion and God
and he himself
are discussed,
these sayings of Jesus
have less chance of being quoted
than that other saying
by one of his critics,
Karl Marx,
who said exactly the opposite
when speaking about religion
and about its followers.
　　He said:
　　"Religion is the
　　opium
　　of the people."
It makes you sleep,
it makes you unaware.
it numbs,
it drugs.
The message of all religious leaders is:
fall asleep,
forget about your suffering
here on earth;
everything will be over
in a world to come.
Religion is a dope,
to prevent people

in this world
from struggling
and from overcoming
all the suffering
they have to undergo.
Some go further
and they ask
why people in this world
suffer so much
if there is a God
    who is all-knowing
    and all-present
    and all-merciful.
Why does God not take
that suffering away?
Why does God not take
all evil away?
Some even seem to suggest
that there is a plot:
a plot between the religious leaders
and those who make others suffer;
a scheme
through which the exploiters
make the exploited
suffer in this world,
so that the exploited may go on
looking up to God
and to those who pretend
to represent God.
    A famous philosopher
    like Bertrand Russell
    wrote
    that he could not understand
    the logic
    of religious believers
    who say:
        "This world is bad,
        all goes wrong,

too much suffering,
too much pain,
and that is why I believe
that there is another world
to come
that is very good."
They reason like that man,
Russell wrote,
who is eating grapes,
very bitter grapes.
He eats the first
very bitter one;
he eats the second
very bitter one;
and the third
even more bitter one,
and the fourth,
and the fifth,
and the sixth,
and who, then, says:
"All those six were so bitter,
that I know now for sure
that the seventh
will be very, very sweet."
    That is why Russell decided
not to be a Christian
and not to believe in God,
because, he said,
God is no help,
and our idea of God
is deceiving;
it makes us unrealistic,
unheroic,
and unauthentic.
It swings us
to sleep.
But Jesus said the contrary.
He said:

"Stay awake."
And he did not say only
stay awake;
he added
that we all should work
to overcome
the evil in this world.
He did not want us
to be drugged.
>He gave us his bread,
>to break it.
>He gave us his wine,
>to share it.
>He gave us his Spirit,
>to live his life.
>He gave us his power,
>to move trees
>and mountains
>and ill will
>and sin
>and ourselves.
If God himself
did all this,
if God prevented all evil
and all suffering
and all mistakes
in this world,
then
we really would be
>asleep
>and drugged
>and lifeless
>and conditioned.
>All risks would be
>taken away;
>all stupidities would be
>avoided;

not by us,
but by God.
And who would *we*
be?
Nobodies,
nobodies,
divinely computerized robots,
puppets on a string,
mechanically dancing
dolls.
Stay awake,
the time will come,
his time will come,
our time will come:
we expect Jesus to return,
we expect Jesus to take over;
he will do that
in two ways.
He will come into this world
from within us,
because with his Spirit
we have to transform ourselves
and this world.
He will come too
from outside,
as our final guarantee,
when his and our work
is over.
Saint Paul believed
that on the last day
those who are still alive
will
GO UP,
and Saint John believed
that on the last day
Jesus will
COME DOWN.

When those two movements
meet,
advent will be over,
and we will be
in him,
humankind
forever and ever.

2.

PRODUCING FRUITS

Matthew 3:1-12

The time of advent
is a time of expectation.
We know, of course,
what we are waiting for.
We are waiting for Jesus Christ
just as the people in the Old Testament
were waiting for him.
> But those people in the Old Testament
> were waiting not only
> for HIM;
> they were waiting also
> for the victory
> he would bring,
> for the gifts
> he was going to offer,
> for the fruits
> of his activity.
They were waiting
for another world,
for a new world,
for another humankind,
for a new humankind,

11

for another justice,
for a new justice.
    In the Old Testament
    those hopes were well described
    by the prophets,
    people who hoped
    so much.
In our time
these hopes
are still better
known
and very carefully described
in a charter
signed by practically all nations
on earth,
on the tenth of December 1948,
during advent time,
the time that all Christians
hope for new things
to come:
the Universal Declaration of Human Rights.
    But who has to bring about
    those new things,
    those new relations,
    that new respect
    in an old society?
    John the Baptist said,
    The man who will come
    after me:
    Jesus.
    But where is
    he?
Yesterday
a cute young girl
of about ten years old
came to ask me
whether she could be baptized.

I asked her:
Who is Jesus?
And she gave,
with a smile
in her very clear eyes
a wrong answer
that was correct.
She said:
    Jesus is the Holy Spirit
    in us.
When we criticize the old world,
when we criticize this world,
our conversations
always seem
to take the same turn:
    students discussing
    the life at the university
    will say
    how lonely they are,
    how dull life is,
    how nothing happens,
    how everyone thinks only
    of himself or herself.
    They say:
    when you come
    you have a circle of friends,
    because you are not the only one
    from your school.
    But those friends
    choose different subjects
    and the circle gets
    smaller
    and smaller
    and in the end
    you are
    alone
    and lonely,

with only *the others*
to blame.
Priests discuss
their diocese,
and they complain:
nothing,
nothing ever happens,
and it is the bishop
and all *the others*
who are to be
blamed.

    Citizens discuss
    national affairs;
    they all know,
    they think,
    what should happen
    and why it should happen,
    but we are all waiting
    for *others*
    to realize our human rights
    and to respect those
    of our brothers
    and sisters.

Long ago
I found in an old yellow booklet
somewhere in a library
the story of the wedding feast
at Cana.
But the book
added something.
It explained
why
there was no wine
that day.

    When those two wanted to marry,
    they wanted to marry
    with a good feast,
    but they were not very rich,

and that is why the families
had decided
to help them
with the drinks.
They had said to each other,
let everyone bring wine,
and we will all pour it
in the empty waterpots
in the kitchen.
So before the feast started
they all came along
with pots
and skins
on top of their heads.
They went to the kitchen
and poured them
into the pots.
When everyone had done so
the master of ceremonies
came to taste.
He took a glass,
filled it
from the pots,
and he tasted it.
        When he put
        the glass to his lips,
        he smiled,
        but that smile
        on his face
        fell suddenly
        away.
        They asked him:
        "What is wrong?"
        He said:
        "It is water only."
They all had been mean.
They all had brought water
in their pots

and in their skins.
They all had thought,
if all the others bring wine,
nobody will notice
that I brought water
only.
They all had left the wine
to the others.
     And that is why,
     the old booklet explained,
     Mary had to go to Jesus,
     saying:
     "There is no wine,
     only water."
The Spirit of Jesus
is given to us.
It is we who should pour
the wine
that has to change
this world.
     The time of expectation
     is over.
     It is up to us
     to start
     to produce the fruits
     that we all expect,
     baptized as we are
     in his Spirit
     and with his fire.

3.

LIFE REGAINED

Matthew 11:2-11

Why
did John the Baptist
end up in prison?
The most commonly heard reason is
that he had condemned King Herod
for his loose
marriage.
But there must have been
a deeper reason.
Herod had been arresting
and killing before.
> The reason must have been
> the whole of John's preaching.
> After all,
> he preached
> the total downfall
> of the existing order.
That old order
was,
as he had shouted,
like an old tree
that was going to be cut
down

17

and that was going to be burnt
in the fire.
What man in charge,
what king,
likes to hear
those words?
　　Once before
　　Herod
　　had already tried
　　to nip in the bud
　　the change to come,
　　when he had ordered,
　　very cruelly,
　　that all the male babies
　　in Bethlehem
　　be killed
　　years before.
John was convinced
that the change
would take place.
That is why
he did not even fear
too much
at the moment
of his arrest.
His stay in prison
might be only
for a few days.
　　Jesus was going
　　to take over
　　anyway.
And so he went to prison.
They took his camelskin off,
and they shaved his head,
and they took his girdle away,
and they dressed him in
a prisoner's garb,

because, they said,
he might try
to lay his hands
on himself.
He started waiting
for the things
he was sure
would happen.
      But nothing,
      nothing happened
      the first week,
      and the second week,
      and the third week,
      the first month:
      nothing.
John got upset,
and he asked some of his disciples,
who got permission to visit him,
to go and ask
Jesus
      when the big crush,
      when the crunch,
      when the big bang,
      when the end
      would come.
They went to Jesus
to ask him,
and he answered them.
He said:
"Go back,
greet him,
and tell him:
      the end did come,
      for the blind see,
      so blindness is over;
      the deaf hear,
      so deafness has passed;

the mute speak,
so dumbness is finished;
the lame walk,
the dead live,
the kingdom is on the way."
If you study
the preaching of John the Baptist,
you will see
that John
spoke almost exclusively
about the total end
of the existing order.
That order would crash
and fall apart.
If you study
the preaching of John the Baptist,
you will see too
that John
thought
that that end
would be the end.
Full stop.
The tree would fall,
the chaff would burn.

It is on that point
that Jesus took over:
the blind see,
the deaf hear,
the mute speak,
the lame walk,
the dead live,
the negative is changed over
to positive.
The end is not only
destruction,
but reconstruction,
a new beginning,
life regained.

It is in that way
that we should prepare
for Christmas
in this country
and in this world.
We should not only be
prophets of doom.
There are already too many
John the Baptists
nowadays.
We should be like Jesus,
restoring,
rebuilding,
invigorating,
regaining.
     All kinds of research
     have pointed to the difficulties
     in this world.
     There are large groups
     of marginal people
     who do not participate
     in the activity
     and the life
     God meant for all.
     There are the handicapped,
     the unemployed,
     the starving,
     the poor;
     there is the rift between
     the rich and the poor;
     there are the political
     and economic problems,
     and so on,
     and so on.
     What to do?
Should we only criticize
and rumormonger
and accuse

and grumble
about the old tree
falling down
like John?
    Let us not forget
    that John
    stood corrected by Jesus,
    who admired John
    very much,
    but who also told
    the others
    that John's time
    was
    over.

4.

JESUS TO BE BORN

Matthew 1:18-25

Christmas is not
the giving of gifts;
Christmas is not
the receiving of gifts;
Christmas is not
the going to a midnight service;
Christmas is not
the singing of Christmas carols;
Christmas is not
the mayor's Christmas tree;
Christmas is not
eating more than you can;
Christmas is
     sharing in what
     happened to Mary
     when she got filled
     with the Holy Spirit.
     But
     how,
       and when,
       and where
       do you get
       filled?

23

Very many believe
piously
that Mary
was at prayer
when the angel invaded
her life.
Luke's text
does not say so.
Was she really
praying?
Very many people
who have been praying
for years and years
in all kinds of ways
sometimes admit
that they never "felt"
the presence of God
while praying.
        Bishop Anthony Bloom
        in his book
        A School of Prayer
        gives the example of a lady
        who came to him
        complaining
        that she had been praying for
        fourteen solid years
        and that she never "felt"
        God's presence,
        nor the presence of God's Spirit
        in her life.
        She came to the bishop
        for his advice.
        The bishop gave her
        his advice.
        After some time
        she came to report,
        and she told him
        what she had done:

she had gone into her house,
she had made herself comfortable,
she had started to knit,
she had felt very relaxed,
and she noticed with deep content
the pleasantness of her room
and the beauty of the garden
she could see through her window,
with the flowers and the birds,
and the people passing through the street
and suddenly . . .
Sometimes I wonder
whether all that restricting
of God and God's presence
to the times of our prayer
is not a device
to get God out of sight
where God really counts.
We allow God to be with us
when we decide to go to church,
or when we fall on our knees
and close our eyes
and fold our hands,
granting God to live only
in the sanctuary,
in the holy of our lives.
We turn the roles;
we make God depend on us.
There was a well-known
Bible scholar
who became seventy years old,
and on his birthday
there was a gathering
in which his friends and students
came to thank him
for all he had done
to make God's word
clearer to them.

And one of his friends
dared to ask him then
why it was
that he,
famous for his biblical studies
all over the world,
had never visited
the "Holy Land,"
Jerusalem and all those
other places
in which Jesus had lived.
His answer was very
deep.
He said:
because I did not want
to risk
making the mistake
of trying to find Jesus
in another situation
and environment
than the one
in which I
daily live
with him
over here:
this is his holy land
for me.
   The Spirit,
   announced to Mary
   so long and far ago,
   wants to be reborn
   in us,
   in our lives,
   as he was born in her
   and in this world,
   while she was at work
   in her kitchen,

in her street,
in her house,
in her field,
in the commonness
of her life
here on earth.

5.

JESUS, THE STRANGER

Luke 2:1-14

There was no room for him
the night he was born
in this,
HIS world.
>Mary must have started her labor
>during the night.
>Joseph must have been very nervous
>about the whole affair:
>he was all alone,
>he had to do all kinds of things
>at the same time;
>he had to fetch water,
>he had to boil that water,
>which meant that he had to light a fire,
>and he obviously did not have
>any matches;
>he had to tear up linen,
>while Mary kept asking him:
>where do we put him,
>where do we put him?
There don't seem to have been
any complications,
thank God.

The baby started to cry in time;
he was disconnected,
washed,
and wrapped up,
and that was that.
 Even when the cleaning was over,
 everything remained silent outside,
 very silent,
 an ominous silence.
 Nobody paid any attention,
 everybody was busy with other things
 in his world,
 because, after all,
 he was born into HIS world.
There were no flags,
no parades,
no military bands,
no salute shots,
no demonstrations,
no processions,
no fireworks,
nothing;
there was not even a baby-cot,
nor a midwife,
not even a grandmother,
a sister or aunt,
nothing and nobody.
 It remained so silent,
 that finally even his Father in heaven
 got nervous about it,
 and he decided to break the silence,
 he himself.
 He sent an angel
 to the people
 who were nearest to the birth,
 to save them transportation costs.
 He sent first one angel
 and later a whole crowd of them

to the shepherds
who slept in a field
nearby.
We have beautiful songs
about those shepherds,
and we make beautiful statues
and pictures of them.
We depict them
as wise old men
talking every day until deep in the night
about the Messiah to come,
studying the Old Testament prophets,
and playing nostalgic tunes
on their violins, bagpipes, and flutes.

>The reality is, however, different.
>Those shepherds in the fields
>were ruffians.
>They were the hired ones
>Jesus would later speak about
>with no concern for their flock.
>According to the rabbinic evaluation
>they belonged
>to the outcasts of society.
>Shepherds were considered
>to be a-social,
>untrustworthy,
>and unsettled:
>they were classed with the sinners,
>the tax collectors, and the prostitutes.

But God's angels went to them,
who had no place in this world
to call their home,
as he had none;
God's angels went to them,
to whom official society
paid no attention,
as it paid none
to him.

God's angels went to them
    and not to the high priests,
    and not to the king,
    and not to the professors at the seminary,
    and not to the businessmen in town,
    but to them, those shepherds,
    who, like him,
    were outcasts and strangers
    and the
    GLORY OF GOD SHONE ROUND THEM.
    They got the message,
    they hurried away,
    they found the child,
    and they praised and glorified
    the Lord,
    while the whole rest of the official world
    was silent,
    asleep,
    and absent.
That Christmas night
God came into his own domain,
to his own people,
but they did not recognize him.
He had become a total stranger
in the world
he had made.
He had started a paradise
with a beautiful Adam
and an even more beautiful Eve,
the unbeatable Miss World Number One,
    but her son murdered
    his brother, Abel,
    and they had turned paradise
    into a hell.
He had started a paradise,
    but they built the tower of Babel,
    and they constructed the atomic
    and the neutron bombs.

He had started a paradise,
> but Joseph was sold by his brothers,
> and the Third World
> by the First and the Second ones.

He had started a paradise,
> but everywhere
> there was murder and war,
> brothers killing brothers,
> sisters killing sisters,
> people tortured,
> manipulated,
> and left alone.

When God
looked around in the world
he had created,
he did not recognize his work
anymore,
and that is why he came back,
and that is why he as a child
was not born,
could not be born,
in any of the structures, buildings,
or organizations of this world.
He was born *in the empty field,*
a complete new start.

> But, brother or sister,
> have we not become strangers
> in this world also!
> Do you feel at home
> in your relationships?
> Do you feel at home
> in this world
> when you read
> *Newsweek* or *Time?*
> Do you feel at home
> when you look around you?
> Do you feel at home
> at home?

Have not we,
ourselves,
become aliens
in this world,
on this earth?
And that is why,
maybe,
we might feel more at home
with him,
in that open field,
where he started
humankind
anew,
with the shepherds,
and maybe,
no, certainly,
his glory will shine around us
too,
around you
and me.

6.

MOST OF HIS TIME

Matthew 2:13-15, 19-23

They settled in a town
called Nazareth,
and there he spent,
with his family,
more than 90 percent
of his life.
  There are no authenticated and canonized
  miracle stories
  about that longest period
  of his stay
  with us.
  We do not know anything
  about it.
  We know only
  that the years passed
  and that he grew
  through adolescence
  into adulthood.
The difference between him
and us
was not made known.
The difference made no
difference.

34

And in a sense
he was in Nazareth
more
God with us
than later on:
>   he lived the type of life,
>   family life,
>   we all know about
>   in one way or another.
>   And yet even then
>   he did not live
>   as we do,
>   because we live in a society
>   where the difference
>   seems almost always
>   to make
>   the difference.
We have to be better
than others;
we have to be the first ones
in our tests,
fighting for
>   grades,
>   certificates,
>   prizes,
>   incomes,
>   and degrees.
In our self-esteem
we depend too much
on those
outstanding qualities
that make us different
from all the others,
and people
who do not have those qualities
look at themselves
in mirrors all over our world
and they see nothing

and they consider themselves
as
nobodies.
 I am the first one
 in my class,
 and we cling like schoolchildren
 to those aspects in us
 that put us
 apart
 from others:
  my skills,
  my techniques,
  my insights,
  my sermons,
  and even
  my religious experiences,
 and we become
  jealous,
  mean,
  anxious,
  insecure,
  envious,
  and hateful,
 and we cannot form
 a community
 with others
 because of all that,
 because we refuse to live
 in a world we have in common
 with others,
 and live,
 or try to live
 within the margins
 of our common
 existence.
It is in Nazareth
that Jesus taught us
that we human beings

do not find our real identity
on those edges
of our human lives
where we can brag
about our specialities
and charisms;
        we find it
        in the center
        of that life
        when we recognize
        our basic human
        sameness,
        where we discover
        each other
        as brothers and sisters,
        cut of the same cloth that
        he, Jesus,
        was cut of.
He did not reveal himself
as our redeemer
so much
by being different from us,
but by being
the same,
with a difference.

7.

A STAR AT ITS RISING

Matthew 2:1-12

It was in the middle of the night,
it was in the middle of their night,
that those wise men
saw a new star
at its rising.
> The Greek text does not say
> that they saw a star in the East.
> The Greek text uses a technical,
> astronomical
> expression:
> they saw a star
> at its rising.
They must have seen
something special
in that star,
that night.
Most probably they believed
like so many of their and our
contemporaries,
that everybody has his or her star.
At the birth of everyone,
a star is born,
the star that determines
our horoscopes.

Some Jewish astrologers
believed that too,
and even in the very pious community
of Qumran
a text was found
with a horoscope
of the Messiah
to be born.
> This star was special.
> It was so special
> that those wise men
> decided that it had something to do
> with a new beginning.
And they,
then and there,
resolved to follow it.
> That must have been
> a crucial decision.
> It meant leaving
> all they had,
> at least for the time being.
> It meant a farewell
> to so much that had been
> dear to them
> up to then.
> But they packed up
> and they went
> to walk behind that star.
> They took certain things
> with them.
> Three of them
> are mentioned:
> > gold,
> > frankincense,
> > and myrrh.
> Those three items
> in those days
> belonged to the most important
> commercial goods

of the regions
they came from.
The Middle East trade
depended so much on them
that John the Evangelist
mentioned all three of them
when he foresaw in his
"book of revelation"
that once the whole world trade
had collapsed:
> "the merchants of the earth
> weep,
> since no one buys
> their goods anymore:
> cargo of gold, . . . myrrh, . . . frankincense. . . ."

After having packed
their camels
with those commercial goods,
they followed that star,
for weeks and weeks,
for months and months,
maybe even for years and years
until the star disappeared
in the dark night
over Jerusalem.
> They tried to get
> some information.
> They asked for the
> new beginning.
> They asked for a
> baby born.
> They asked for the
> new king of the Jews.

The whole of old Jerusalem
was shocked
and shaken.
They did not expect any newness.
At least the king did not,
the scribes did not,

the scholars did not,
and any other people in power
did not either.
They did not even want to expect
anything
new.
They lived too much
on the situation
as it was.
     But once through Jerusalem,
     the star again appeared;
     it stopped at Bethlehem,
     and they found the child
     and his mother,
     and they delivered their goods,
     all the things they had.
     They handed them in,
     they fell on their knees,
     and they worshipped him
     as the center of their new lives.
They left their gold
and its trade,
the frankincense
and its production,
the myrrh
and its consumption,
behind at the manger,
and they returned home,
different men,
by a different way.
     They were the first ones
     to trade in all they had
     to be with him,
     a child,
     who later on in his life
     would point at another child
     to indicate
     the type of life
     he came to bring.

8.

A LAMB MISUNDERSTOOD

John 1:29-34

When John saw
Jesus coming,
he pointed at him
and said:
        "Look,
        there is the lamb of God,
        who is going to carry
        all the sins of the world."
And he added:
        "The Spirit of God
        is
        on him."
But to his listeners
it must have sounded
like a curse,
because they knew
the lamb
he was compared with.
It was the lamb
that in their tradition,
but also in the traditions
of so many African peoples,
was slaughtered

or sent into the wilderness
after having been loaded
and charged
with all the sins
of the community
in which it had been
growing up.
>It is a lamb
>that can lead
>to very many
>misunderstandings.
Some theologians developed a theory
in which God the Father
became a kind of revengeful,
bloodthirsty,
if I may say so,
monster,
demanding,
clamoring for
the blood of his son.
According to them,
he wanted to see blood,
the blood of that lamb.
>Brothers and sisters,
>it is not true.
>God does not want to see
>that blood.
>God does not want to see
>any blood
>at all.
>Even in the responsorial psalm
>of today,
>God makes that very clear.
>God does not ask
>for sacrifices
>and holocausts;
>God does not ask
>for a victim.

From the very beginning
God has been interested
in only one thing:
our well-being.
God created us to live
and not to die.
God's will is the well-being
of humankind
and NOTHING else.
God's kingdom is the kingdom
of human life.
You may call it grace,
you may call it salvation,
it all comes to the same;
God wants us
to live.
It is that interest in human life
and nothing else
that makes up
the Spirit of Jesus,
because it is
the Spirit of God.
He was not just a lamb
on which humankind,
on which you and me,
can put our hands
to unload
our sins
or something like that.
He said:
"I came to bring life,"
and that is what he did;
he got Lazarus from his grave
and that boy in Naim,
and that other girl.
He said:
"I am the light of the world,"
and that is what he was:

he made the blind see
and the ignorant understand.
He said:
"I am the life of the world,"
and he gave the hungry bread to eat,
and the thirsty to drink.
He did not complain,
when they had no wine,
but he,
the greatest party-goer of all time,
gave them 900 liters of wine
to drink.
He did not only say to his followers,
you should be responsible;
he gave them ALL responsibility,
he gave them HIS Spirit,
so that they could be responsible
by themselves.
    He was not a mere lamb
    who fished them out
    of the troubled waters
    of this world
    to get them high and dry,
    safe and saved.
    He told them to go out
    to change this world.
    He told them to overcome
    all the powers of death
    in this world:
        jealousy,
        envy,
        hatred,
        pettiness,
        racism and tribalism,
        poverty and misery,
        torture and violence,
        greed and lust,
        sickness and death,

as he overcame them
all.
We should not misunderstand
God
because of that lamb;
we should not misunderstand
Jesus
because of that lamb;
we should not misunderstand
ourselves either
because of that lamb.
We have the terrible
and deadening possibility
of doing that,
to look for another
to get rid of our responsibility:
We are greedy
because others are greedy;
it is their fault
not mine.
We drink ourselves senseless
because society around us
is frustrating;
it is the fault of society,
not ours.
We run around with prostitutes
because the campus is unsocial;
it is the fault of the campus,
not mine.
We have a baby
without any family organization,
because we feel so lonely in this world;
the fault is the world's,
not ours.
We bribe and we steal,
we throw away food,
because, we explain,
we live in a bribing and stealing
and wasting society.

We speak about the rift
between the rich and the poor,
we enjoy it when others speak about that
too;
we listen and we applaud,
but how do we relate to
the sweepers and the cleaners,
the janitors and the nightwatchmen,
the poor among,
in the midst of us?
We have our lambs,
our scapegoats,
for all we do.
One very faithful follower
of Jesus said
that as long as in this world
one person cleans the toilet
of another person,
this world is no good.
       The man who said this
       is a man who changed in his days
       the face of India,
       according to the method of Jesus,
       by giving himself
       nonviolently
       in the interest of all:
       Mahatma Gandhi.
We should be lambs
like Jesus,
and in no other
way.

9.

THE NEW ALTERNATIVE

Matthew 4:12-23

When Jesus heard
that John the Baptist
had been arrested
he knew that his time
had come.
>The greatest and
>the last prophet
>of the old order
>had finished
>his mission.
>A new world was going
>to start.

He left his home,
walked into the crowds
alongside the lake,
and he announced
without any further ado:
"The kingdom of heaven
is very near,
it is close at hand."
And in fact
that kingdom broke through
only some minutes later

48

when he called Simon and Andrew
to leave their nets.
They did.
A few moments later
James and John did
the same,
leaving their father Zebedee
behind
in his boat
alone,
with the help
only of the men
he employed.
> Those four stepped over
> from their old life
> into a new one;
> they stepped over from one family,
> the one of their fathers in those boats,
> into a new family,
> the one of their Father in heaven;
> they stepped from one social order,
> the one based merely on environment
> and human interaction,
> into a new one,
> the one based on Jesus' call;
> they stepped from one type
> of economic activity
> into a completely different life.
And that changeover,
that conversion,
was from that very beginning
not only something passive,
a mere following,
a mere discipleship,
a mere intellectual or moral
attitude
stuck on top of the rest
of their lives;

it was at the same time
a task
and a mission:
they got something
to do.
　　Jesus said:
　　　"Follow me,
　　　and I will make you
　　　fishers of men."
　　Just as he would have said,
　　if they had been masons:
　　　"Follow me
　　　and I will make you
　　　builders of humankind."
　　Or engineers:
　　　"Follow me
　　　and I will make you
　　　bridge-builders
　　　between human beings."
　　Or doctors:
　　　"Follow me,
　　　and I will make you
　　　really heal the sick."
He introduced,
that afternoon,
his alternative world.
We all know
how much
we need such a world,
even to be able to control
the most physical threats
to our life.
　　　We need an alternative world
　　　to be able to combat the plague
　　　that is not only threatening
　　　this town and this country,
　　　but is killing people
　　　who are our neighbors.

Why are there the fleas
that infect human beings
with that dreadful disease?
Because there are rats
in whose furs those fleas
are breeding.
Why are there rats
that carry those fleas?
Because there is
misery
and poverty,
squalor
and dirt,
neglect
and waste.
    The Bible always uses
    the pest
    as a sign
    that something went wrong
    in human relations,
    and that an alternative,
    more just
    lifestyle had to be worked
    out.
Why are the locusts
threatening Kenya
at the moment
in their trillions
and trillions?
Is it not because
the human relations
in that part
of the world
are spoiled
and because people
are fighting
and doing nothing
about those insects,

though they know
that they are a threat
to all they have
and to all they are.
          The appearance of locusts
          was in the Bible seen
          as a sign of God's wrath
          because of sinful
          human relationships,
          and this is now,
          in our modern times,
          even more true
          than ever before,
          because if the relations
          in Ogaden*
          had been good,
          we could have killed
          those locusts,
          long, long ago.
Why are there wars,
armed robberies?
Why is there starvation,
thirst,
soil erosion,
lack of rain,
lack of medicine,
schooling, textbooks,
and justice?
          We need an alternative world,
          and that is why Jesus
          entered the scene of this world,
          of this country Kenya,
          and he said:
          "Follow me
          and I will make you
          into builders
          of a new earth."

Through him
heaven broke
into this world.

*The Ogaden is a region in Ethiopia where, while this sermon was given, a war was going on between Somalia and Ethiopia. Because of that war, the international anti-locust organizations had not been able to eradicate the locusts in one of their traditional breeding places: the Ogaden desert. The locusts breeding there threatened to invade Kenya, a country bordering on Ethiopia.

10.

HAPPINESS DID START

Matthew 5:1-12

Good news is bad news,
and really bad news
is good news indeed.
         If I go
         to one or another office
         in this university
         and I am treated well,
         and the administrator I need
         is polite
         and kind
         and understanding
         and helpful,
         then I have nothing to tell
         my secretary
         when I get back to my office.
         She will ask:
         "Any news?"
         And my answer will be:
         "No,
         everything is okay."
But if I go to an office
in this university

and the administrator I need
is only a big, pedantic,
proud stink,
and he shouts at me,
and I shout at him,
and finally we shout together,
then I have quite something to tell
my secretary
when I get back.
    If you get a phone call
    —let us hope it will never come—
    with really bad, very bad news,
    then you will be able
    to organize around you
    without any difficulty
    a group of willing listeners
    who listen exactly up to the moment
    that they know your story,
    and after that
    they run away
    as fast as they can
    to tell it to as many people
    as they can.
    Bad news is good news
    indeed.
    And while they run,
    the terribleness of that news
    is even growing.
But if you get a phone call
to say
that all goes well,
then you might even ask
your caller:
"Did you really phone me
to tell me that?
Who is interested in hearing
that all goes well?"

We like to hear scandals
and we love to be able
to tell them.
The real news
is the bad news:
>How do you do?
>Very well,
>but . . .
>>it is there that
>>the news starts.
The papers we read
know that too,
the *Daily Nation,*
the *Standard,*
the *Nairobi Times,*
Trust, Drum, and *Viva*:
their main stories
are almost always
about
>crime,
>rape,
>disease,
>death,
>murder,
>robberies,
>arrests,
>and policemen who shoot
>others
>straight through
>their hearts.
We seem to love bad news,
we thrive on bad news.
Journalists turn up
in great numbers
only when things go wrong.
And the more those things go wrong
the greater their number
will be.

Around Jesus
it seems to have been
the same.
Check the Gospels.
They are called:
good news.
But listen to what he, himself,
tells them:
    the king an immoral man,
    the tax collectors
    and administrators
    hopeless,
    the men adulterers,
    the whole lot of them
        —they ALL left when he said
        if anyone of you is
        without that sin,
        let him stay—
    his best friend John detained,
    the shepherds, hirelings and mercenaries,
    housewives losing their money,
    children neglected, scandalized,
    sick or dead,
    the occupying forces murdering people
    even in the temple,
    the priests hypocrites,
    the disciples unundersanding,
    Judas a traitor,
    the only tower mentioned
    falling over and killing
    a lot of people,
    sons lost,
    sheep in the wilderness:
    How do you do?
    Very well,
    but . . .
It must have been
in that context

that Jesus
in the Gospel reading of today
climbed out of that world
onto a hill
to have a better view,
and it was in that context
that he said:
    "Listen,
    listen carefully!
    We are deceiving ourselves.
    There is happiness,
    notwithstanding all the stories
    we tell;
    there is hope,
    things are going on,
    the kingdom of heaven
    is establishing itself.
    Look around you,
    anywhere:
        look at the gentle ones,
        the comforting ones,
        the pure ones,
        the outgoing ones,
        the ones who do not stick
        to what they have.
        Think about all the help
        given to brothers and sisters,
        sick people and helpless people.
        Look at the peacemakers,
        the merciful ones,
        the seekers of justice,
        the strugglers for wholeness.
        Happiness
        everywhere."
We tell each other stories
about doom
and corruption,

about bribes
and smuggling,
about the big fish
that go wrong,
and about the small fry
swimming in their wake.
That is what we say,
but HE said:
   "Do not forget
   what is going on
   really;
   do not forget
   that I, Jesus,
   dared to entrust myself
   as a baby with a frail human body
   and a wide-open baby-skull,
   to the human relationship
   between Mary and Joseph,
      happy,
      comforting,
      merciful,
      peaceful,
      and persecuted only
      in the cause of right."
Let us pray
that that Spirit,
which you can find
anywhere,
will grow
and that it will overgrow
all the bad news
in this world.
Amen.

11.

OF THE EARTH
AND OF THE WORLD

Matthew 5:13-16

We are supposed to be
the salt of the earth
and the light of the world.
Those texts are very well known
and therefore, maybe, also
very often
minsunderstood.
     Christians will say,
     when using these texts:
     "We are the salt,
     we are the light."
     And they do not seem to realize
     that to be salt,
     just like salt,
     is a pretty hopeless affair.
     There was only one person
     in the Bible,
     a lady,
     who really could say:
     "I am salt."
     That lady was the wife of Lot,

who turned into salt,
when she looked back
on her past
in Sodom and Gomorrah.
She became salt,
100 percent salt,
and nobody around her
seems to have been too happy
about it.
To be salt is
hopeless.
There is nothing so unhandy,
so unmanageable,
and so inedible
than salt on its
own.
You can't do anything
with salt alone;
in a time of famine,
you cannot eat it;
in a time of drought,
you can't drink it;
it only would make things
worse.
Salt alone is no good;
it makes the fields unfertile,
it kills life,
it preserves death,
it is heavy
and useless.
It becomes useful
only when it is used,
as Jesus indicates
in the text of today,
mixed up with other things,
and he explains as well
how we should be mixed up.
We are not salt;

we are the salt of the *earth*;
we should be mixed up with the *earth,*
we should be mixed with the reality
around us.
If Christians say or think:
"I am the salt of the earth,"
they should understand
that they should be prepared,
as a consequence,
to be thrown in the cookingpot
of our human affairs.
They cannot stand in front of the pot.
They have to be put in that pot;
they have to be taken;
they have to be mixed
with the contents in that pot;
they have to be boiled and smothered
with it;
they have to go all through it;
they have to simmer with it,
practically disappearing in the process,
but, nevertheless,
making it all
tasty
and palatable.

    Christians who are the salt of the earth
    will not need,
    in the very first place,
    to do all kinds of special things,
    though they might sometimes be called
    to do just that;
    they do not,
    in the very first place,
    have to join all kinds of organizations,
    though they might do that;
    they do not have to organize,
    in the very first place,
    all kinds of prayer groups,
    though they should pray;

they do not even have to do,
in the very first place,
all kinds of social work,
though that is very useful.
Christians who are the salt of the earth
should,
in the very first place,
be tastegiving
    in our human reality,
    in this world,
    in this life,
    in this university,
    in this campus,
    in their hall of residence,
    in this town,
    in their street.
As long as salt
is not mixed,
it is too salty,
it is too bitter,
it is too sharp,
it is too biting,
it is too wounding,
it is too hot.
If salt is taken
too much apart,
then it is like the salt
policemen use
when they punish
small boys picked up
in the street,
who get two or three strokes
with a whip
through a towel
drenched in salt
that is put over their bare
buttocks,
and that salt is beaten
into their live flesh

and it hurts for days
on end.
Salt alone
is unbearable,
it is harmful.
>   And then Jesus speaks
>   about that light
>   we are supposed to be.
>   And again very many Christians
>   will call themselves,
>   eagerly,
>   THE LIGHT.
>   They stand in their own light,
>   just like a candle
>   in an empty room;
>   just like a light
>   put under an empty bucket
>   stands in its own light only,
>   glorifying in its own shine.
Light alone
is useless too.
Light alone
is blinding.
Light alone
does not make you see
anything at all.
Light alone
is used
in the eyes of prisoners
to make them confess.
Light alone
hurts.
>   It becomes of use
>   when it makes us see
>   other things than
>   itself:
>   the world around us.
>   It becomes of use
>   through us,

when it corresponds
to what Jesus said of it:
you are the light of the world.
We should make things visible,
we should light up possibilities,
we should brighten up
our world.
That is our task
and our mission.
Everyone of us
who was baptized
got for that reason a candle,
lit from the Easter Candle:
"Receive the light of Christ."
And in the older baptismal ceremony,
it was for that reason too,
that everyone got
a pinch of salt
on his lips.
    We should be the salt,
    but not apart;
    we should be the light,
    but not on our own.
    If we live and act like this,
    like Jesus Christ,
    then we will be
    light in the darkness of this world
    and taste in its flavorlessness.
    We will be a consolation
    to others;
    we will be
    their salvation,
    their hope,
    and their comfort.
It is that salt,
it is that light,
that you can find,
thank heavens
and thank God,

all over this world,
all over this country,
all over this town:
people hit and changed
by Jesus' Spirit:
>they are lights in the darkness for the upright,
>they are generous and merciful and just,
>they take pity, they give and they lend,
>they conduct their affairs with honor,
>they will never waver,
>they will be remembered forever,
>they have no fear of evil news,
>with firm hearts they trust in the Lord,
>with steadfast hearts they will not fear,
>open-handed they give to the poor,
>their justice will stand forever,
>their heads will be raised in glory.

12.

THE OLD ENEMY

Matthew 4:1-11

He had hardly been known
up to the moment
of his baptism
by John.
    Before that he was
    as well known
    as you and me
    by our family,
    and some friends.
Nobody paid any special notice
to him.
When he passed in the street,
he passed in the street.
When he broke his bread,
he broke his bread.
When he gave his opinion,
he gave his opinion.
When he sat on a donkey,
he sat on a donkey.
    But, then,
    at that baptism,
    suddenly,
    it all changed.

Some learned people
say that it even changed
for Jesus,
that he, himself,
had never known either
who he was
before that baptism.
I don't know,
I don't know
how they know.
But definitely
the others had not known,
and now,
suddenly,
they knew,
because his Father
revealed him
at the moment
that he stepped
in the water
in front of John the Baptist.
Heaven opened,
a voice was heard,
the Spirit was seen,
the Spirit was seen
on him.
He was revealed
in all his power,
with all his authority,
with his mission
to change this world
into another one.
And his first reaction
was
to run away,
to hide,
to put his head
into desert sand,

like an ostrich
does
in danger.
He stayed in that desert
for forty days,
and then that Spirit
that had driven him into it
drove him out of
that desert
again
and his life
in public
began.
    And immediately
    he was tempted,
    not only then
    but all through his life
    by temptations that are known
    to any one of us
    with some
        skill,
        authority,
        insight,
        education,
        power,
        or influence.
Any graduate
who gets a job,
any teacher,
any secretary,
any boss,
any specialist,
any lawyer,
any director,
any doctor,
and anyone among us
has those very same
temptations.

The old enemy said:
"Use your skill and power
and all that,
to get bread,
to get the dough that bread
is really made of:
money."
    And Jesus said:
    "But bread is not all."
    And the tempter said:
    "I agree,
    but it is my most
    common trick,
    and the most common
    fall."
The old enemy put him then
on the temple-top,
and he said:
"Throw yourself
into these temple-affairs,
and angels will carry you
and people will applaud you."
    But Jesus said:
    "You should not put
    God to the test."
    And the tempter said:
    "I agree;
    it is the mistake
    I made myself,
    but many others still do;
    I only tried."
He put him then
on a mountaintop,
and he showed him
all the political powers
in the world,
and he said:
"What about this?

If you don't fall for money,
if you don't fall for honor,
then at least
fall for the thing
they are all falling for:
fall for
political power."
   But again Jesus said:
   "No.
Not this world,
not the actual world."
And he looked at Satan
and said:
"Because, indeed,
it is too much yours
   with its military budgets,
   with its atomic bombs,
   with its life-killing,
   national-security-priority lists,
   spending 10 billion silver coins
   on bombs,
   saying:
   we are never going to use them,
   and forgetting that those bombs
   are, nevertheless,
   exploding in the faces
   and in the lives
   of the millions and millions
   of human beings
   who have no food,
   and no shelter,
   and no education,
   because the money
   was nationally and internationally
   spent
   on those
   bombs
   that kill.

Not this world,
but another one
full of justice
and integrity,
 full of unalienated
human life
and dignity."
 Again he looked at Satan,
that Prince of Death,
and he said:
"I came to save,
you know;
I came to redeem,
you understand."
We all will be tempted
as he was;
or better,
the other way round:
he really was tempted
as we are,
as Saint Paul would remark.
Money, money, money,
is the name of the game;
honor and glory,
OUR honor and glory
without any alleluia
or praise the Lord;
power, political power,
gunpow(d)er.
And if we give in,
this world will not change
insofar as we are concerned,
and we will not be with him,
insofar as he is concerned:
he will forgive us,
he will understand,
he was tempted too,

but we will be
the dead wood
in this world,
which he carried
on his shoulders
on his way
to the cross.

13.

TO OPT UP AND OUT

Matthew 17:1-9

He was not only
tempted to use
his power,
his influence,
and his family relations
for himself alone.
He was also facing
that other temptation
of the religious human being:
the temptation
to live piously
in retreat
from this world.
The temptation
to opt up
and out.
      That morning
      he climbed a mountaintop.
      Peter,
      James,
      and John
      accompanied him.
      They got higher and higher,
      the air got fresher and fresher,

you did not smell
any village anymore,
nor any town.
No smoke of a fire,
no cocks crowing,
no children's voices,
no soldiers,
no police.
Nothing was heard
except their voices
when they talked.
And then
he started to shine.
It started with himself;
the fatigue disappeared
from his eyes,
his feet lost their bruises
and scars,
his hands opened up,
all callouses dissolved,
the dust fell out of
his hair,
he started to shine
like the sun,
and then his clothing
was transformed too,
it looked whiter
than any white
in the light.
No patch,
no stain,
no dirt
any longer:
white and bright
like the sun.
     He was home,
     with his Father
     in heaven,
     with Moses and Elijah.

And then the tempter came.
This time it was
Peter,
and that tempter
said:
    "This is beautiful,
    this is joyful,
    this is alleluia
    sister,
    this is alleluia,
    brother,
    this is it,
    this is it,
       let's keep it,
       let's hold it.
       I will build here
       a house for you,
       a house in stone,
       a permanent residence
       in this light,
       in this glory."
The temptation
to opt,
very piously,
up
and, via a mountaintop,
out of
this world.
    Some time ago
    the North American bishops
    expressed their concern
    about the ever growing
    number of retreat-
    and such like houses
    very often used
    as shelters
    against the realities
    of a Christian life
    in this world.

Jesus did not even
so much as say a word
to his tempter.
Without paying
any attention
to Peter,
he discussed with Moses and Elijah
his passover,
his way of the cross,
his death,
and his chore
in this world.
>And he descended
>with them from there,
>from the fresh air
>up there,
>into the foul air
>below,
>from the light
>up there,
>into the shadow
>down here.
>He descended
>into the world
>he had come for.
We should follow him up
to the mountaintop;
that is what he asked
Peter, James, and John
to do;
but we should follow him
too
down again.
>Let us not live
>opted up
>and opted out.
>Let us not create
>a pietistic vacuum
>around ourselves.

Let us be
like him,
engaged in this world,
progressive
and alert.
Let us follow him
up,
let us follow him
down.
There is no
other way
to his home
with the Father.

14.

THE THIRST AT SAMARIA

John 4:5-42

The story seems to be
a simple
man-meets-woman,
boy-meets-girl
story.
    It is the type of story
    you find in literature
    again and again:
    a man,
    a hero,
    a shepherd,
    a leader,
    arrives at a well
    and meets a woman
    who came to fetch water:
        there is the caring hand
        of a woman,
        the helping hand
        of a man,
        and everything that follows
        thereafter.
In the Bible
the story is told
several times.

Abraham,
wondering about how to get
a wife
for his son Isaac,
sends one of his most trusted servants
out
to his original home-country
to look for that wife.
>   The servant arrived at a well,
>   he made his camels kneel down
>   waiting for the evening
>   for the time that the local girls
>   would come to draw water.
>   Before they come,
>   he prays:
>>   "God of Abraham,
>>   here I stand at this well,
>>   where the women will come
>>   to fetch water.
>>   God of Abraham,
>>   I will ask those women
>>   to give me a drink,
>>   and the one who cares
>>   that will be the one."
The women do come,
he asks for a drink,
Rebecca obliges,
immediately he brings out his gifts,
golden earrings and a ring in her nose,
the affair is settled
forever after.
>   There is the story of Jacob,
>   looking for a wife.
>   He meets Rachel at a well,
>   a well that is covered
>   with a heavy stone lid.
>   The stone is so heavy
>   that one has to wait

until sufficient people
are together
to be able to take it away.
But when Jacob sees Rachel
he is in his admiration
suddenly so powerful,
that he, to his surprise,
can lift the stone
alone.
Moses defended
the seven daughters of the priest Reuel
against the shepherds of the region
harassing those girls
at a well
in the desert of Midian.
He married one of them,
Zipporah,
as his wife.
The fourth story
is the one at Samaria:
Jesus asking for a drink,
and a woman from Samaria:
asking him
for the living water
that will quench her thirst
once and for all.
The lady has no name;
John does not give her a name;
she is representing humankind
when asking her question,
all of us.
The first story
was a love story.
In the second story
Jacob helps Rachel.
In the third story
Moses defends those seven girls
as their savior.

In the fourth story
things are getting more involved.
Salvation as such is discussed,
words like MESSIAH
are mentioned.
    "Please, Sir,
    help us, we are thirsty.
    Give us the living,
    eternal water.
    If you are the redeemer,
    let us drink."
Redeemer and redemption,
savior and salvation,
what do those words mean?
That is a very difficult
and a very much discussed question.
What is the redemption we are looking for?
    There is the answer of those
    who reduce Jesus' message and mission
    to piety:
        peace of mind,
        being washed in the blood
        of the Lamb,
        all personal sins are
        taken away;
        I am saved.
    There is the answer of those
    who reduce Jesus' message and mission
    to a social calling:
        it is about the poor,
        the abandoned, the disabled;
        it is about justice, equality,
        brotherhood, and development.
        He is to be found
        not in piety,
        not in praying fellowship-groups,
        but in the inner-city slums,
        in South Africa,

in the plantations of
South America.
Both groups have their difficulties.
The first group,
the group of the pious interpretation,
have no difficulties
with their Christian identity.
They know what it means
to be a Christian.
They know what makes them different
from the others.
They are ready to witness to this
day and night.
That is not their difficulty;
their difficulty is their relevance.
What is the relevance, the meaning,
of their piety to others,
to Africa,
to the world,
to the oppressed and the poor?
    In the second group that relevance
    is no difficulty.
    They are relevant to the communities
    they live in.
    They are willing to work
    for the emancipation of the poor.
    They join in literacy programs,
    they will do all kinds of things like that.
    They have difficulties with their
    Christian identity.
    They are doing things
    others are doing too.
    The others are very often
    doing those things even better than they.
    It is within this frame of mind
    that it is sometimes said
    in a country that becomes socialist:
    we have no need of Christ.

What to do?
What should be our stand?
What was that lady,
standing in
for the whole of humankind,
really asking for?
>It was a redemption
>in very many fields:
>she had no water,
>she had no husband,
>she asked about religion.
>Redemption should take place
>in all those fields.

Redemption in the economic field:
It is here that the poor come in;
redemption in this world
has to take into consideration
that our differences are too great;
the poor are starving
while the rich are overeating.
>And Jesus said:
>"Break your bread."

Redemption in the political field:
In many countries,
in almost every country,
maybe in all countries
political power is not shared;
it is too often used only
to oppress others.
>And Jesus said:
>"There should be no master among you."

Redemption in the cultural field:
All over the world cultural minorities
are oppressed.
Women are treated differently
from men.
The rights of children
are overlooked.

And Jesus took a child
and put it in the center
of his group.
Redemption in the ecological field:
We should be liberated
in such a way
that the world,
our earth,
is going to be liberated
too;
so that animals and plants,
pure water and fresh air
survive with us.
            And Jesus said:
            "Look at the flowers . . ."
Redemption in the field of final meaning:
But even if all the above redemptions
had taken place;
if this world were just,
respectful to all,
assuring equal rights
in a healthy environment,
one final question would remain:
"So what;
it all leads to final
death."
            Our struggles,
            our sufferings,
            our efforts,
            and our lives
            should have a lasting meaning,
            if only to enable us
            to find the courage to be
            and to go on.
It is here that we should look
at the cross.
Not because the cross
is the end.

But exactly because the cross
is not the end
after all.
He rose to that new life
that is the only
satisfactory answer
to the question of that lady
at Samaria.
    We, Christians,
    participating in his Spirit,
    should be redemptive,
    together with Jesus,
    and therefore with the Father in
        the economic,
        the political,
        the cultural,
        and the ecological fields.
But we should know as well
that being together with him
in all that,
we will be led
to a cross,
where the old world
will die.
We need to want that death,
to be able to be with him,
the fundamental sense-maker
and meaning-giver,
Jesus Christ,
forever and ever.
Amen.

15.

HE BEGAN TO SEE

John 9:1-41

First there was that lady
in Samaria
who had no name.
He promised her
that she would
see.
This Sunday
there is that man,
a blind man,
nameless like her.
He was standing in front
of Jesus,
but he did not see;
he was blind.
> We all know what a blind man
> looks like.
> We all know how he
> behaves,
> because if you are not
> blind yourself,
> you saw him stumbling
> here or there.

87

A blind man is
surrounded by his world,
by the things he needs.
Everything is there:
>   his room,
>   his table,
>   his chair,
>   his bed,
>   the handle on his door.
But he does not see.
It is that man
Jesus met in the street.
Jesus saw him:
he did not see Jesus,
just as he did not see
>   the children,
>   the girls,
>   the trees,
>   and the flowers.
Jesus took some of
the mud
that the whole of humankind
originally
was made of,
according to the Bible.
>   He put that fresh mud
>   on the old eyes
>   of that nameless
>   blind man,
>   and suddenly
>   HE saw
>   everything:
>   not only Jesus,
>   the children,
>   the girls,
>   the trees,
>   and the flowers.

He saw much more,
because we hear him
almost immediately
involved in discussions
with the authorities
on God,
on the sabbath,
on sin
and signs,
on Jesus
and his belief
in the Son of man.
He saw it all,
and they drove him away,
because while he saw,
they remained blind.
Very many things
could be said
about a text like this,
especially when it is written
by that mysterious author
John.
Let us take one
striking aspect
only.
That man said:
"*He*
put mud on my eyes
and now
I see."
He was in the dark
and now he saw
for himself.
In the situation
of this world
we all lived
in the dark.

And then Jesus stepped in
and he said:
"I am the light
of the world."
A light
that is going to clarify
all.
That is true
and it is not true.
     He
     came as the light
     into this world
     so that
     we
     might see.
That sight is given
to us.
That sight is lacking
among us.
Lord,
make
us
see,
and, like that man,
judge
and act.

16.

DEAD AND BURIED

John 11:1-45

This is the last Sunday
of Lent.
The first Sunday we saw
Jesus tempted by Satan
to think of himself alone.
The second Sunday Peter
tempted him
to opt up and out.
The third Sunday
a thirsty lady
represented the whole of
humankind.
The fourth Sunday
he made a nameless man
see
for us all.
This last Sunday
his friend is introduced.
He has a name,
he has our name:
LAZARUS,
and that means:
"helpless."

When the report starts,
Lazarus is
dead
    —though Jesus suggests
    that he is only
    asleep—
and buried.
He is completely
bound up,
strings around his arms,
cords around his legs,
two stones on his eyes,
his mouth gagged,
a cloth around his head,
lifeless in a tomb
with a stone in front
and the smell of decay
inside.
    Does Lazarus,
    too,
    stand for
    us?
Is that what the blind man
saw
at the moment
he started to look
around
in this world?
Is that not,
what
WE
too
would see
when we look
around
in our world?
    Humankind is
    like that man
    LAZARUS,

helpless,
frustrated,
bound up,
smelly,
decaying,
blind,
deaf,
at a loss,
full of maggots,
dead.
That is how Jesus
found his friend,
that helpless man,
Lazarus,
a man he had loved
so much.
When he got Lazarus' smell
in his nose,
it got in his eyes as well.
First there was a knot
in his throat,
but then that lump
came up
and he wept,
he wept bitterly,
and they said:
"Look how he loved
him."
He said:
"Roll that stone
away."
But his sister said:
"Do not roll that stone away,
leave things as they are,
the smell would be
unbearable."
Just as we so often say:
"Let's not touch
this or that issue;

it might explode
in our face."
He said:
"Roll that stone
away,"
and he called him:
"Lazarus!"
and he commanded him:
"Come out!"
    And that dead man
    came out
    and started
    to live.
Jesus wants to do
to us,
to humankind,
what he did to Lazarus.
    Let us step
    out of the tomb.
    Let us get the bonds
    from our legs and arms,
    let us get the stones
    from our eyes,
    and the cotton out of
    our ears and mouth,
    and let us live
    with him.

17.

PITY TURNED ROUND

Matthew 26:14-27:66

When we hear or read
the story of his passion,
we feel,
of course,
pity for him,
who carried his cross,
because he wanted to undo
that whole sinful order of things
that has trapped us
in our tombs—
      A tomb dug
      by technicians,
      authorized
      by the political powers,
      and blessed and sealed
      by high priests.
We have pity
on him.
And in that apparently
most pious of ways
we are trapped
again,

turning it all
around.

> It is the one mistake
> he himself corrected,
> even while carrying his cross.
> When some women bewailed
> HIM,
> he stopped,
> he turned around,
> and said:
> "Do not weep for me,
> weep for yourself,
> weep for your world,
> weep for Jerusalem."

He carried that cross,
because he had pity
on us.
He carried that cross,
because he wanted to liberate
us.
He was arrested,
because we are arrested;
he was going to die
because we are dead.

> He is the high priest
> who understood
> and experienced
> our human lot
> in a world
> as we made it.
> He is the high priest
> who has pity
> on us,
> alienated as we are
> from the life
> that was his gift.
> He took that alienation
> upon himself

as it was
and
as it is.
He allowed himself
to be caught by it,
to be bound by it.
He let all the powers
that diminish and bind,
that exploit and enforce,
that deceive and lie
have him.
He let them do
what they could.
He let himself be
    arrested,
    spit at,
    detained,
    tortured,
    ridiculed,
    and killed.
But after that death,
he opened his eyes,
not blind anymore;
he opened his hands,
not bound anymore;
he stretched his body,
not kept anymore;
he opened his mouth,
not gagged anymore,
and he said:
    "I have passed
    through it all.
    Evil,
    where is your power?
    Satan,
    where is your might?
    Death,
    where is your sting?"

Let us have no pity
on him;
let us have pity
on ourselves,
still unbound,
notwithstanding
his liberation.

18.

THE EMPTY TOMB

John 20:1-9

Yesterday afternoon
I went to buy some bread.
The girl in the shop
asked me,
"Don't you want
any cake?
It's Christmas
tomorrow."
The man at the cash register
interrupted saying:
"It's not Christmas,
it's Easter."
And then she said:
"It's all the same,
it's about something
new."
> That conversation
> was not very much of a
> theological discussion,
> and yet,
> something
> very true
> was said.

It was even said
during the Easter vigil
last night.
That Easter celebration
started with the
story of creation,
a new birth:
> man was born,
> woman was born
> in beauty and splendor,
> in goodness and wholeness.

But something happened
to all that beauty,
a worm started to gnaw
at all that splendor,
a sin
interfered.
Death crept
in.
Human beings
all over the globe
have been trying
to understand
that ununderstandable
development.
> An African way of
> touching upon this mystery
> is the story
> of that old woman,
> sometimes called Leda.

She was beautiful and vigorous,
she walked straight up
and everyone looked at her
when she swayed through
the village.
But then God
beset her.

Her father died,
dried up like a stick
in the sun.
Her mother died,
bony as a basket
swinging from a branch.
Her husband died,
bleached like a fishbone
on the shore.
And she cried:
"I wish it had never
become today.
God called him too
quickly.
My father was old,
true,
my mother was old,
period,
my husband was not old
at all.
God give him water,
he had not even time
to drink.
God make a fire for him,
he is so cold."
Her oldest child died,
dehydrated like a dead little bird.
She took her youngest child
in her lap,
at her breasts,
against her heart,
between her thighs,
and she pleaded:
"Don't take this one;
he is my life,
he is my support;
don't take this one;

who would carry me
when I am old?"
But he too
died
in her arms.
    And then she stood up
    in her full length,
    and she shouted
    at heaven:
    "Give account,
    give account!"
And she started to build a tower
of wood
to reach
that God.
But when the tower
was very high
it bent
and broke.
    She started a new one
    stronger this time,
    but when it was high
    it bent
    and broke.
She looked around
and saw how
at the horizon
heaven touches
this world.
She said,
"That is how
I can reach
him too."
And she started to walk
toward the horizon.
And she walked,
and she walked,
the whole world round,

and she walked,
and she walked,
until people started to laugh
when she passed
again and again.
They asked her:
"Where are you
going?"
She explained,
and they laughed louder,
and they said:
"Do you think
you are different
from us?
We are all the same.
It happened to
all of us."
> But she went on walking,
> until,
> but that is not the old
> African story
> anymore,
> she was one of the women
> at the tomb
> on that Easter morning.
> And that tomb
> was empty . . .
and she understood
and believed.
ALLELUIA!

19.

THOMAS'S DOUBT

John 20:19-31

Thomas is a difficulty,
even liturgically,
because he turns up,
again and again,
every year
on this second Sunday of
Easter.
     Though a saint,
     his name is used
     in such a way
     that his holiness
     seems to be
     "in doubt."
To be called
a Thomas
is not so very good,
because Thomas was
the doubter.
     Some other aspects
     in the life of Thomas,
     even the ones recorded
     in the Gospels,
     remain most times
     overlooked,

because of his hesitation
at Easter.
But when, for instance,
the others doubted
whether they were going
to follow Jesus
to Jerusalem,
where he was going
to die,
it was Thomas who said:
"Let us join
and die
with him."
What did Thomas
doubt really?
Was it the resurrection
of the Lord,
or was it the attitude
of the others?
They said that
they had seen him;
they said that
he had eaten with them,
but they were just sitting
there,
waiting for a new
appearance.
They did not give
any sign,
as yet,
that this resurrection
meant anything at all
in their lives.
Life seemed to go on
as always.
Was it because
of this
that Thomas did not believe

that they had been
confronted with
the risen Lord?
Martin Buber,
the famous Jewish philosopher,
tells a story of an old rabbi
who every morning,
after getting up,
sent his servant
to the window
of his sleeping-room
to see
whether the Messiah
had arrived
in this world
over the last
twelve hours.
　　That servant saw
　　every morning
　　hundreds of Christians
　　in the street
　　going from home
　　to their work,
　　coming from church
　　to their homes.
　　They all believed,
　　officially and formally,
　　that the risen Lord
　　had been seen
　　and was with them.
But it did not seem
to make any difference
to them.
And that is why
the servant
had to answer
every single morning:

"No,
not yet,
no sign of him."
    When Thomas
    saw his Lord,
    he fell on his knees
    and he said:
    "My Lord and
    my God."
His life was changed
from that day on
totally.
    He believed in deed,
    where others were
    doubting
    in fact.
    Aren't we?

20.

OUR OWN HOPE

Luke 24:13-35

The two from Emmaus
walked with Jesus.
He spoke with them
about himself;
they spoke with him
about himself.
    They said:
    "Sir,
    you really should have seen
    the signs
    he did
    in the sight of God
    but also
    in the sight of the whole people."
    They said:
    "We had hoped
    so very much
    that he would have
    liberated us,
    but now it is already
    two days ago
    that he was crucified

and nothing seems
to happen
at all."
They walked on with him,
and he explained
the whole of Scriptures;
he edified them,
because later
they would say
that their hearts
had been
burning
all the time
he spoke.
        They got tears
        in their eyes
        when they understood,
        but nevertheless
        they did not
        recognize him:
        the Son of God.
They asked him
to feel at home
with them.
They asked him
to stay,
because, they said,
it is getting
dark
and there are robbers
everywhere.
He stayed.
They went on talking,
but then
he took HIS bread,
he broke it
to share,

and then they
suddenly
saw,
and notwithstanding
the darkness
against which they had warned
him
only a few minutes
before,
they stood up
and returned to
Jerusalem.
>   For almost two thousand years
>   we Christians
>   have been walking
>   together
>   with millions and millions
>   through this world
>   from our Jerusalem
>   to our Emmaus.
Those others walked
with us,
and we talked
very often even
about him,
and we built churches,
and we built seminaries.
They asked us
to stay
with them,
because, they said,
it is getting darker
and darker
in this world.
>   And then we stopped talking,
>   and we showed in very many signs
>   that we wanted to share with them;

we built
    clinics
    and schools
    and orphanages
    and rural and other
    training centers
    all over the world.
It is true that
very many
recognized
in all that work
God,
Jesus Christ,
and their Spirit.
    And yet,
    it seems
    that we left too many questions
    unanswered
    and too many hopes
    unfulfilled.
    They say:
    "We had hoped so much
    that you would be the ones
    to set the world free;
    two thousand years
    have gone by
    since it all
    happened."
        When we speak about
        setting people free,
        when we speak about
        liberation and a
        pass-over,
        we cannot but remember
        that other liberator
        sent from God:
        MOSES.

It is in the life of
Moses
that we hear
how two things
can be done
in times of oppression
and need.
    The daughter of Pharaoh
    did one of the two
    when she fished Moses
    out of the Nile
    and in fact
    out of death.
        That is all she did,
        and she will be remembered
        because of it
        up to the end of times.
        The oppression,
        however,
        remained.
But the one
she had fished
out of that river
would work
with God
in a more radical way.
He changed it all.
    Are we in the church
    not too often
    content with doing
    the thing
    the daughter of Pharaoh
    did,
    and are we not too often
    too lax
    to do
    what Moses
    did?

We are willing
to share
as she shared.
Are we willing
to share
as Moses shared,
or better still
as Jesus?
If we would break
our bread
as he broke his,
how could we not be
recognized
as his?

21.

HE IS THE OPEN DOOR

John 10:1-10

Did you
as a child,
or worse,
as an adult,
ever step out of your bed
on the wrong side
in the middle
of the night?
      It is a horrible
      experience,
      because you are
      completely disorientated.
      You are looking
      for the light switch;
      it is not there.
      You are groping for the window,
      for the small stool
      next to your bed,
      for your shoes,
      for the door.
      You can't find
      any of them,

114

and you start to scream,
to scream
for that door:
the door,
where is the door?
Until someone hears you
and comes
to open that door
and to bring some light.
The door alone
would not be sufficient.
You must be able
to open it.
  A French philosopher,
  Jean Paul Sartre,
  wrote,
  long ago,
  a theatre-play
  about four persons
  locked up in one room.
  There is a door
  in that room,
  but it is closed
  and the whole situation
  turns into hell,
  sheer hell.
    You must have heard stories
    about caves
    that fell in;
    about doors of freezing rooms
    that closed
    behind somebody;
    about car doors
    that would not open anymore,
    and about the panic,
    the hunger and the thirst,
    the isolation and desolation.

But it is not only
in this physical way
that people can be blocked
or barred.
We can be barred
in so many ways,
        by a sickness,
        by a rule or regulation,
        by a complex or trauma,
        by our family and friends,
        by a car and a house,
        by what we own
        and by what we believe.
All those things can lock us
in and up;
we are hemmed in,
and we don't know
what to do,
how to escape;
there is no exit,
no gate,
no door.
        And then
        there is that man
        from Nazareth,
        who says:
        "I am the door";
        and who
        at some other time said:
        "I have opened a door
        in front of you,
        a door
        nobody will be able
        to close."
For thirty years
he had lived in Nazareth;
nobody knows
what he did over there;

most probably
the usual things.
But then
he escaped,
he was free,
and he set others
free also:
>the paralyzed man
>who came through the roof
>because the door was blocked,
>was told:
>>"Your sins are forgiven,
>>your legs are unbound."
And the leaders
did not like
that.
>Levi, the tax collector,
>who was sitting in his office
>straight up
>in his money and
>in his intrigues
>was told:
>>"Follow me,"
>>and he stood up
>>without counting his money
>>and the cost.
And the leaders
did not like
that.
>They were all fasting,
>he was not fasting,
>they were all sticking
>to an absolute Sabbath-rule,
>>but he healed
>>that day.
And the leaders
did not like
that either.

They preferred
to keep all doors
closed.
So many in our world
think,
like those leaders
in his time,
that things are settled,
that we are caught
once and for all.
So many think
that our situation
is desperate,
without an escape hatch,
shut in on itself,
but he said:
"I AM A DOOR,
I AM THE DOOR"
leading us from
the restrictions of a world
so familiar to us
into space,
into God,
into transcendency,
but also into a kingdom
here on earth,
into him
who said:
"I was hungry
and you gave me to eat;
I was thirsty
and you gave me to drink";
in all the senses
of those words.

22.

TO TAKE YOU WITH ME

John 14:1-12

The report on Jesus
today
seems to be a very well known
story.
It has happened very often
before.
You must have heard it
a dozen and more
times.
> There is that location,
> somewhere up-country,
> full of poverty
> and misery.
> The rain does not come,
> and if it comes
> it washes all
> away.
> The harvest does not grow,
> and if it grows
> there are no roads
> to transport
> it.

119

The local school is
no good,
and even if you succeed
you cannot go on.
The houses are too small,
without much more than
one room,
a room that instead of
protecting you,
embarrasses you
more than anything else.
And then there
arrives that man,
that man
coming from town,
who says:
"Do not let your hearts
be troubled.
Trust in God,
but better still
trust in me.
There are many rooms
and houses elsewhere
in town.
If they were not there
I would not be speaking
about them,
now.
I am going there
to prepare
a place for you.
After I have gone
and after having prepared
you a place,
I shall return
to take you with me,
so that where I am
you will be too.

But of course
I cannot travel on foot.
I cannot travel
on an empty stomach,
so please,"
      and he takes
      his hat,
"be generous,
    so that I can go."
And his hat goes around
and all sacrifice
what they can,
and he walks away
and the people in the village
wave and wave,
and he disappears
at the end of the road,
and they do not see him
anymore.
Off he is
and they start
to wait,
and people die,
and they still wait,
and people grow up,
and they still wait,
and nobody does anything
about their misery and squalor,
about the houses and the schools
because they say:
      "He will return;
      he said
      there are plenty of rooms
      and he knows
      because he comes
      from there."
Brother and sister,
not you,

but how many others
are not saying exactly that
about that Jesus of Nazareth,
who said:
"I go
to prepare you a place,"
and who
never
came back?
    And all kinds of people
    because of that promise
    refuse to overhaul
    this world,
    or don't find
    sufficient motivation
    to do something about
    the situation
    of the global village
    in which we live,
    over here.
If that is
the whole message
of Jesus,
we
over here
are really deceived
and misled,
especially because he too
disappeared
and was no longer seen
when he passed
on his road
into heaven,
into the sky,
the last cloud,
to prepare for us,
as he said,
a room
over there.

We have been waiting
for almost 2000 years;
in fact,
humankind
has been waiting for very much
longer,
because,
before he came
we had been waiting
for him
for ages and ages.
He came
but he went off
again,
and therefore,
O brother and sister,
let us pray,
very hard,
that he may return
very soon
to take us with him
to that heavenly town
with all those rooms,
alleluia,
Amen.
And that could be
the end of this sermon
because Jesus
is, of course,
not
like that man from town.
Jesus can be trusted;
he will come.
Let us wait
in hope and faith
with charity.
    But how could this
    really be
    the end of this sermon?

It is true
that Jesus said
that in his Father's place,
in the heavenly city
JERUSALEM,
there are very many rooms.
But speaking about those rooms
and those dwelling places
we should not overlook
that other set of texts
in John:
   "If anyone loves me
   he will keep my word,
   and my father will love him,
   and he will come
   to him
   and make a dwelling place
   in him."
And that dwelling place
is NOT in another world;
it is
IN US
here and now;
   and with him in us
   and with the Father in us
   and with the Spirit in us,
     we are supposed
     to keep his word,
     and his word
     says
     that
     we should do
     "good works,"
     even
     "greater works
     than he did,"
     not over there
     in heaven,

but over here
on earth,
in this world,
overcoming
the squalor and the misery,
the poverty and the hunger,
the poor schooling
and the lousy situation.
"I tell you
most solemnly,
whoever believes in me
will perform the same works
as I do myself;
he will perform even greater works
because I am going to the Father
and *whatever* you ask for
I will do it,"
in this world,
and so much has to be done
and so much can be done
by us
with him.

23.

JOHN'S SECRET CODE

John 14:15-21

There are, as you know,
very many situations
in which authors
or journalists
cannot write
what they would like to write,
because if they wrote
what they would like to write
they would be writing
their last words.
    Because of this,
    authors and journalists
    have developed techniques
    to indicate, nevertheless,
    in between the lines
    what they want to say.
    They quote others,
    they play with words,
    they use hidden meanings,
    and for those who are informed
    the message comes through,
    notwithstanding all restrictions
    and censorships.

126

When you read a Gospel
like the one of today
you get the impression
that John does the same.
He wrote long after the death
of Jesus Christ,
and when you read him
you do not find the directness
of Luke
or Mark
or Matthew.
When John speaks about Jesus
it sounds different.
     It is
          complicated,
          mystical,
          mysterious,
          idealistic,
          and almost ununderstandable.
     It is just as if
     he were using
     a secret code.
He speaks about a knowledge
some have,
and the ·world has not
and will never have.
He speaks about
words
and works
and love
and truth
and a Father
and commandments,
about coming
and going,
about taking us up
and about leaving us
over here.

It is all so highly intricate
that some Bible scholars
even say
that we should forget about John,
that he is not really an evangelist,
but a gnostic author,
that is to say,
an author
who wrote only
for a very small group
of "converts"
or "saved ones";
he did not write
for us,
the common Christians,
the "idiots,"
which really means:
the common people.
And then they close
his book
and forget about it.
I believe in the Jesus
of Mark,
    yes;
I believe in the Jesus
of Luke,
    yes;
I believe in the Jesus
of Matthew,
    yes;
but in the one
of John,
    no.

    They believe in the Jesus
    who met the common men and women
    in the streets
    and on the roads,

but not in that Jesus
of the Gospel
of John
who speaks
endlessly
in a small hall
during the evening hours
to a small group
of elected ones.
But I wonder
whether it is wise
and correct
to do away with John
just like that.
I even wonder
whether John
is all that mystical.
He does not seem to be
that mystical
at all.
He speaks about *love,*
true,
but that love
seems to consist in
the keeping of the commandments;
he speaks about *words,*
true,
but he says that we should
do
the works
Jesus did.
He speaks about that Jesus
being the Son of God,
but he mentions also
that Jesus said
that we *all* are
SONS OF GOD (10:34).

We are all the sons
and the daughters of God.
That is why
we should be
like Jesus,
who is the Son of God
and consequently
we should be
like God,
HIS and OUR Father.
In a certain sense
this sounds very mystical,
but it is really not mystical
at all.
Karl Marx said
that we Christians
are a useless lot
because we only look
at the Father
and pray to him.
But John says
that Jesus said
that God said
that we should NOT look
at him,
but that we should BE
like him.
What does it mean
to be like
that Father,
or as some very modern
translations read:
to be like that
PARENT,
GOD?
To be a Father,
to be a parent,
means to give *life*.

That is what God did
when he created
us.
That is what his Son did
when he walked with
us.
That is what his Spirit did
when it descended into
us.
That is consequently
what we should do:
give life,
enlarge and strengthen life,
take care of it,
so that it is good,
healthy,
satisfactory,
free and
open.

> Do you know
> where Jesus' quotation
> that we are
> SONS OF GOD
> comes from?

It is taken from Psalm 82.
In that psalm God is presiding
in the assembly
of the "Gods,"
and he gives his verdict:

> "YOU MUST STOP JUDGING
> UNJUSTLY,
> YOU MUST NO LONGER BE PARTIAL
> TO THE WICKED.
> DEFEND THE RIGHTS OF THE POOR,
> OF THE ORPHANS,
> AND THE HELPLESS;
> RESCUE THEM
> FROM THE POWER OF EVIL MEN."

And then God,
sitting on his throne,
judging the "Gods"
      —and we are those "Gods"—
continues:
      "HOW IGNORANT YOU ARE,
      HOW STUPID;
      YOU ARE COMPLETELY CORRUPT
      AND JUSTICE HAS DISAPPEARED
      FROM THE WORLD."
And he goes on:
      "YOU ARE GODS,
      I SAID,
      ALL OF YOU ARE THE SONS OF THE MOST HIGH,
      BUT YOU WILL DIE;
      YOUR LIFE WILL END
      LIKE THAT OF ANY
      PRINCE."
That will be our end
if we do not give life,
real life,
to our own children
and to all children
in this world.
      If we do not give life
      we are doomed;
      if we do give life
      in the way God and Jesus
      gave life,
      we cannot be doomed
      because we are
      plugged in
      to life divine,
      according to John's
      deciphered secret
      and sacred
      code.

24.

HE DID NOT STAY

Matthew 28:19-20

Today we commemorate the fact
that Jesus disappeared.
We do not only commemorate
that departure;
we even celebrate it.
We have a feast
because he got away.
That is rather strange
if you come to think
about it.
When a loved person
dies,
or is reported
missing,
this hardly ever
is a cause
for celebration.
You do not call
your friends together
when your wife or husband
dies
to have a good party,

a jolly drink,
a nice piece of meat,
and things like that.
> When a loved one
> disappears,
> there is not only
> sadness,
> but shock,
> and nobody knows
> what to do.
Some days ago
I was confronted
with such a death
in a family.
She was preparing
a meal
for her guests
at five minutes past eight PM,
she was dead at
a quarter past eight PM.
She had already set
the table,
the plates
and the spoons,
and then all at once
she was not there
anymore.
> But the table was set,
> and the spoons were still there,
> as she had put them,
> and nobody knew
> whether they should take
> them away
> or leave them there.
We are, nevertheless,
according to a very old custom
in our Christian communities,

invited to celebrate
the ascension,
or disappearance,
of the Lord,
because,
      —as he said himself—
      it is good for us
      that he is away.
      Why is that?
      On the eighth of May
      in the year 1808
      a child was born
      in a small German town,
      about 170 years ago.
      He was originally a Jew
      and his name
      is almost as well known
      as the one of Jesus.
      His name was
      Karl Marx.
      When he was eighteen years old
      he went to a university,
      the University of Berlin,
      and six years later
      he handed in his thesis
      for his Ph.D. in philosophy.
      In that thesis
      that very young man
      wrote
      that a philosopher
      has only ONE vocation,
      and only ONE task:
      to combat the Gods.
He did not write:
"to combat God";
he wrote
"to combat the Gods."

He wanted to fight
anything or anybody
that would make people think
that they should bend their knees
or bow their heads,
in front of something
or someone else,
forgetting about
their own dignity.
The people who pray
to God
and expect
all from God,
Marx said,
are alienated people.
They are strangers
in their own lives.
They do not take themselves
seriously.
But the people
who adore their car,
that trinity of
oil, iron, and rubber,
and who dance
in worship around it,
also have
an alienating God
in their lives;
and students
who take their examinations
more seriously
than their own health
and the health of their children
are in the same
difficulty.
     The accusations of Marx
     are serious,

and if you understand him well,
even very noble
and understandable.
And yet,
he is wrong
when he thinks
that *our God*
is the danger
he is thinking of.
Jesus left us.
He did not hang on
like a father
who gives his business
to his son,
but comes to check him
in his office
every day.
He did not hang on
like the expatriate businessman
who had to hand over his business,
who did hand it over,
but who really did not do that;
he brought in
his own stooge
and business is as
usual.

    Jesus did not do that;
    he went away,
    more thoroughly
    than any one of us
    will leave this world
    at death.
    He took *all* with him,
    his bones,
    his hair,
    his teeth,
    and his heart.

And before he left,
he said:
    "Now it is up to you;
    go and preach,
    work and change
    this, your world,
    into the kingdom
    of God."
Be baptized
in the belief
that God the Father
gave you
life.
Be baptized
in the belief
that Jesus Christ
revealed what
you can do.
Be baptized
in the belief
that you, yourself,
received
his Spirit.
    The Easter candle
    that has represented
    the risen Christ
    among us
    since Easter
    is going to be blown out
    today.
    He is no longer
    with us
    in that way.
    The flowers
    in front of it
    should now
    be placed in front of us;

with his Spirit,
you can do anything,
you can do it,
we can do it.
Let us do it!

25.

THE SPIRIT WE RECEIVED

John 20:19-23

The feast of Pentecost,
the feast of the sending of
the Holy Spirit,
is in a sense
the only feast in the liturgical year
that is really ours.
    The other feasts
    are all about
    what happened
    to others,
    to Jesus:
        his conception,
        his birth,
        his baptism,
        his life,
        his transfiguration,
        his death,
        his resurrection,
        his ascension;
    to Mary,
    to Joseph,
    to the Apostles,
    and to all the saints.

140

Today we celebrate
a mystery
that happened
to us,
to his followers.
At least
that is the intention
of this feast;
we can even now
act
as if
it is all about others
only.
> A theologian
> who understood
> that danger
> very well
> was a Lutheran minister,
> Søren Kierkegaard,
> more than a hundred years
> ago.
> He held
> that most Christians
> are not Christians
> at all.
> They only talk
> about it.
>> When the bishop of his diocese,
>> Copenhagen,
>> died
>> and when everybody
>> in the press
>> and everybody
>> at his graveside
>> spoke,
>> in glowing terms,
>> about this great
>> Christian,

Kierkegaard noted in
his diary,
something like this:
   "He is dead now.
   And as he has been
   responsible
   for a very long period,
   it would have been desirable
   that one would have been able
   to convince him
   to end his life
   by giving in to
   Jesus Christ,
   and to admit
   that what he represented
   among us
   was not Christianity,
   but a compromise."
He explained what
he meant
in his sermon
about the geese.
   He compared his fellow Christians
   to domesticated geese.
   Those geese are always
   talking about
   flying:
   "We have wings,
   we never use our wings,
   we should use them,
   let us fly."
   But nobody ever
   flies.
   On Sundays
   a big goose
   stands a bit higher
   than the other ones
   in a pulpit,

and he too,
every Sunday,
exhorts the others
to fly,
in the most beautiful
words.
But nobody does fly,
and if one would start to fly
the preacher himself
would be
the first one
to shout:
"Come down
immediately."
Pentecost
is our feast,
it is the feast
of our take-off
with the Spirit.
With that Spirit
we have to fly in
all directions.
    That is another difficulty:
    that variety
    in the Spirit.
He was given at different times:
the third day,
the fiftieth day,
and every day
since.
He was given in different ways:
he blew over them,
and fire descended over them,
and they got him in
noise, light, and smoke.
He was given in different gifts:
    in the gift of peace-making,
    in the gift of forgiving,

in the gift of preaching,
in the gift of tongues,
in the gift of healing,
in the gift of administering,
in the gift of
    dancing,
    singing,
    playing,
    and praising the Lord.
The diversity is so great
and the consequent difficulties
so alarming,
that even
while we are celebrating
all this
today,
    Paul is quoted,
    from a letter by him
    to Corinth,
    where the group of Jesus'
    followers
    threatened to be split up
    because they were all
    flying in different
    directions.
But they,
over there,
in Corinth
were at least flying.
It is to those fliers
that Paul wrote:
    "There is a variety of gifts
    but always
    the same Spirit.
    There are all sorts of services
    but always
    to the same Lord.

There are all kinds of ways,
but it is the same God
who is working
in all."
Let us belong
to those
who fly
on the wind
of that Spirit,
and let us fly
together
into the dawn
of his kingdom
to come.

26.

OUR GOD

John 3:16-18

At Pentecost
we commemorated
how the Holy Spirit
imploded in us.
The small flames
that were seen
over the heads
of his disciples
disappeared
INTO
those heads
and
INTO
those disciples
to help them
to live.
At Pentecost
we celebrated
in a way
ourselves.
     And it is
     as if the liturgists
     responsible

for all the feasts
we celebrate
regret
that they allowed us
last week
to concentrate so much
on ourselves,
because today
we are asked
to think of God alone
in that very own life of his,
the life of the
blessed Trinity.
Three persons in one,
the nature of God,
who understands all that?
Nobody.
And that is why
this feast
seems to be an occasion
you can best celebrate
with your nose
in a book
by one or another
African theologian,
who proved to be good
at the theology
of that Trinity:
    Augustine,
    Tertullian,
    or Cyprian.
But if we forget
about that theology,
if we forget
about those persons
and that one nature,
that unity and that trinity,
that oneness and plurality,

and if we only look
at the *names,*
then
that God of ours
proves to be nothing
silent and mysterious
in itself.

He is a FATHER,
not only of his Son,
but of us as well,
and that Son of his
is consequently
not only a SON
but our brother as well,
and that SPIRIT of theirs
is the same Spirit
that works in us.

Our God is not something
or somebody
static,
like a photo;
he is like a motion picture.
Our God is
dynamic,
he is charged,
he attracts,
he does not stay home,
he does not remain within God-self,
he relates,
he gives life.

The feast of the blessed Trinity:
Father,
Brother,
Spirit,
is not the feast
of God;
it is the feast of
OUR GOD.

27.

SHARING ONE LOAF

John 6:51-58

The last evening
that Jesus was free
to be with his disciples
he shared his bread
in another way
than he had been sharing it
with them before.
He handed his cup around
in another way
than he had been handing
that cup
to them before.
Why this double up,
why this extra
during a meal
he himself
had provided
for them?

      Very many theologians
      have told us
      that it is very difficult
      to penetrate the psychology
      of Jesus;

they all say
that he remains
a greater mystery
to them
than any other person
they know.
But do those scholars
belong to the class of people
Jesus belonged to?
And if they don't,
how would they be able
to know?
    The official theologians
    over the centuries
    and even nowadays
    were most times
    priests and monks
    who lived rather apart
    from those places
    in the world
    where real human life
    is lived.
        They have been living in convents
        and monasteries,
        in the ivory towers
        of universities,
        pastoral institutes,
        and theological colleges.
    They met
    each other;
    they talked with
    each other;
    they wrote for
    each other;
    they read
    each other,
    and they discussed
    each other.

They did not have
too much contact
with the type of people
Jesus was seen with:
    the sinners,
    the hungry,
    the poor,
    the children,
    the girls at the well,
    the thirsty,
    and the man and woman
    in the street.
Only once
a theologian
came to Jesus,
and he came
during the night
not to be seen
by the others.
    How would those theologians
    be able
    to understand
    the psychology
    of a man
    who so obviously
    had another interest
    in life
    than they had?
They did not only
not understand Jesus;
their lack of understanding
also colored
the world
they were experts in:
theology.
    Studying this bread and wine,
    this body and blood
    issue,

they studied it
too
within their own
theological context.
They studied
that body and blood
as it lay safely
locked up
in their tabernacles
and their churches,
behind thick, safe,
jewel-studded,
gilded doors.
They studied
that body and blood
as it became present
during their Masses
and as it was adored
during their benedictions.
They explained
the reality of Jesus
in that bread
and in that wine
in all kinds of ways.
They invented theory
after theory,
transubstantiation,
transfiguration,
transymbolization,
and so on.
And you just start
to wonder
whether that is
what Jesus meant
when he took
that bread
and
that cup
and said:

            "Take,
            this is me,
            really,
            eat it,
            drink it,
            be like me.
            I am giving
            you my life,
            live my life
            together."
Jesus incorporated
in that bread
and in that wine
his body
and his person
        not to keep it
        locked up
        in that bread
        and in that wine
        but to share
        through them
        his life,
        with us
        together,
        to form
        with him
        one body
        and one person:
            we form one single body
            because we have all
            a share
            in one loaf.
When we celebrate
this feast of his body,
CORPUS CHRISTI,
we should not restrict
this feast
to that bread
and that wine,

but we should think
about the one body
we are supposed to form
together
through that bread
and wine.
     The question is not *only*
     and maybe not even *mainly*
     whether he is present
     in the bread and the wine
     of themselves
          —he really is—
     the question is *also*
     and maybe *mainly:*
     is HE really present in us
     after we have shared
     that bread and that wine
     with him?
If he is,
we will be seen
sharing our bread and our wine
with others,
as he did
during that very last
meal.
And he added that
extra way,
that double-up,
to enable us
to do
exactly that.

28.

NOT THE SHOUTERS
BUT THE DOERS

Matthew 7:21-27

You all must have heard
about those martyrs of Uganda
about a hundred years ago.
There were very many of them;
twenty-two were Catholics,
twenty-three were Protestants,
and two were Muslims.
They died in different ways;
some were speared,
some were beaten to death,
but most of them
were burnt
on the third of June,
1886.
They were not killed
like sheep
after their mass arrest.
They were arrested
upon their formal declaration
that they
wanted to follow

155

the new way
of Jesus.
They were not numbed
or stupid
after their arrest.
They resisted
all attempts
to make them fall back
into their old ways.
One of them,
Mbaga Tuzinde,
was the son of the chief-executioner,
a man called Muhajanga.
Mbaga had been baptized
on the morning of the day
of the arrests.
His father took him home
for a week
to change his mind;
he did not succeed.

    While the fire was burning
    with thirty-one bundled up boys,
    aged between fourteen and twenty-five,
    in it,
    the executioners
    danced around the pyre
    shouting:
        "It is not we who are
        killing you;
        Nende is killing you,
        Mukasa is killing you,
        Kibaka is killing you,
            the spirit guarding the Eastern frontier
            the great spirit of the Lake,
            the spirit of the war and the storm,
            are killing you."
And the boys
from within the fire
shouted:

"If that is true,
you are their slaves,
you are not free.
You are their slaves,
and we are free."
      They were free
      to escape
         from an older order
         in which they did not
         believe any more.
      They were free
      to live
         in a new order,
         in a redeemed and saved
         order,
         the world of Jesus.
But, brother or sister,
we should not say this
in a way
that
the fight
between old and new
is only a fight
between an old God
and a new God,
between Christ
and the anti-Christ,
high up in the sky
of our ideas
and ideals
on an a-political
and unworldy
battlefield.
      It is a fight
      between the old and the new
      in *this* world,
      in *this* life.
      I don't know exactly
      how to say it,

but when you read
reports on South Africa,
for example,
then it seems
that Christians over there
refuse to analyze
the real situation,
the real political situation
of the oppressed people,
because their fight
is in the air.
Their fight is an ideological
struggle
between Christ and the anti-Christ,
between the West and the East,
between Christianity and Marxism.
The economic,
social,
and political
struggle of millions
and millions
is reduced,
or elevated,
to a fight between
Christ
and Satan.
In the Gospel of today
Jesus says:
"It is not those
who say to me,
Lord, Lord,
who will enter
the kingdom of heaven,
but the person
who does the will
of my Father."
Before he said that,
he had indicated that will
very clearly:

he had started with
the beatitudes,
but after that
he had spoken about
   law,
   anger,
   adultery,
   divorce,
   vows,
   revenge,
   enemies,
   charity,
   prayer,
   fasting,
   justice,
   and human relations
—all things to be done
in *this* world.
Our fight is not in the air,
between ideas and ideals.
Our fight is here and now
as it was there and then
for those martyrs
who refused
to cooperate
any longer
with things at the court
of that king,
because they knew them
to be unjust.
   It is not those
   who shout,
   Lord, Lord,
   Christianity,
   Christian culture,
   Church, Pope, or Bishop
   who enter the kingdom,
   but those who do
   the will of God,

refusing a bribe,
taking up a child,
establishing justice,
because they have that faith
in Jesus Christ
that will justify them
and their world.

29.

WORSHIP AND EXODUS

Matthew 9:9-13

While Jesus was walking
he saw a man
called Matthew,
a tax collector,
a collaborator,
a representative of the oppressive
Roman colonial power.
He was sitting in front
of the custom house
receiving tax
and the obligatory extras
he himself
freely added.
Jesus said to him:
"Follow me,"
and Matthew got up
and followed him.
Up to that moment
Matthew
had not been
a free man.
He was a colonized one;
he had been domesticated
by the oppressors of his people;

he had to sing their tune,
and he had to express
continually
his loyalty to them,
to enemies
of his own people
and of himself.
        Matthew
        was also unfree
        in another way.
        He was a sinner;
        he was bound
            by his money,
            by his career,
            by his deceit,
            and by his lies.
Matthew was so bound up
from without
and
from within
that he could not do
what he wanted to do;
he could not define
his own priorities
really.
        And then that Jesus
        comes along;
        he picks Matthew
        from the small circle
        in which he was living;
        he invites him,
        he does not force him,
        but he invites him:
        follow me,
        get out of your strange prison,
        straighten things out,
        live the life you want to live,
        come.

AND HE CAME,
he followed him,
he got out of the hands
of the Romans,
he got out of the bonds
of money,
a real
EXODUS.
He started a new life,
the one of Jesus,
liberated,
redeemed,
saved.

    That exodus-reality
    is very important
    in the life of Jesus,
    and it should,
    therefore,
    be very important
    in our lives too.
You know
how Jesus waited until Easter
to die;
he instituted
the sacrifice
we are celebrating
at this very moment
during an Easter meal.
    At Easter the Jews,
    and Jesus was one of them,
    celebrated the fact
    that they got out of Egypt,
    where they,
    as you all know,
    were exploited,
    colonized,
    beaten,
    and cheated.

With God's help
they marched
out of their trouble,
out of sin,
out of injustice,
out of being unfairly taxed
in the direction
of a promised land.
When Jesus ate
for the last time
with his disciples
before his pass-over,
he was commemorating
what God
had told the Jewish people,
who were paying taxes
to a cause foreign
to them:
"Get up
and follow me."
It was in that
"exodus"-spirit
that he died on the cross
and gave
his last supper
to us.
We should,
therefore,
today
be celebrating
an EXODUS
out of all those kinds
of bonds and chains
that we call sin
and that are catalogued
day-in-day-out
in the press
of this world.

Is our celebration
such an exodus?
Do we get up,
like Matthew,
and follow?
Liturgy
can be celebrated
in a way
that it is something
completely
different.
Worship
can be organized
in a way
that it offers
no exodus at all,
that it is a consolation,
and a letting off
of steam only,
a reason to do
nothing
at all.
 The very famous
 West Indian
 Frantz Fanon
 once wrote
 about the way
 in which colonized people
 dance
 and celebrate:
  "At a fixed hour
  and at a fixed date,
  men and women
  get together and
  under the attentive eye
  of the tribe,
  they lose themselves
  in a pantomine,

which looks rather like chaos,
but which in fact
turns out to be
a very systematic
headshaking,
bending of the back,
throwing up
and backwards
of the body . . ."
And then
he explains
how those people
get rid of their frustration,
their violence,
and their aggressiveness
in that way.
He adds that that dancing
has an economic function.
When they come,
they are tense,
upset,
impatient,
and in despair;
after the dance
they go home,
released,
satisfied,
calm,
peaceful,
and willing
to undergo more.
    We, too, can
    celebrate
    this liturgy of ours,
    this exodus-commemoration,
    this death and resurrection,
    this "new life,"
    this "get up
    and follow me,"

in a way
that it resembles
that dance,
as described
by Frantz Fanon:
    we get up,
    we sit down,
    we genuflect,
    we stand,
    we kneel down,
    we beat our breasts,
    we bow our heads,
    on the very same spot
    all the time.
We should, however,
get up
and follow
HIM,
who,
because of his pity
and mercy toward us,
wants to lead us
out of the headlines
of the Egypt
in which we live,
together
with him
and that man he called
today:
Matthew.

30.

FIRST CAST OUT, THEN CURE

Matthew 9:36-10:8

The Gospel by Matthew
is often called
the Gospel of our mission.
No Gospel is so outspoken
about what we should
do
as his.
  Last Sunday we saw
  how he,
  Matthew himself,
  was called:
  "Come,"
  and sent:
  "Follow me."
Today the group
is larger;
they are twelve
  —Matthew being
  one of them—
and they get power
to cast out
and to cure.

They were sent out,
not
because he, Jesus,
wanted them
to be *rich*.
On the contrary,
he told them:
"Give without
charge,"
because we all
received without
being charged.
They were sent out,
not
because he, Jesus,
wanted them
to *profit*
from this world
as much as possible.
On the contrary,
he told them
not to take
anything
with them.
They were sent out,
not
because he, Jesus,
wanted them
to *rule*
this world,
but to serve
it.
He sent them out
because he, Jesus,
felt sorry
for the *crowds,*
who were (and are)
without help and lost,
sick and diseased,

harassed and dejected,
terrified and frustrated.
>He sent them out,
>and he gave them power
>to cast out
>unclean spirits
>and to cure.
>In that order:
>>first:
>>*cast out;*
>>second:
>>*cure.*
He did not ask them
to organize
a social assistance organization
only,
>that cures
>the sicknesses,
>the hunger,
>the thirst,
>the diseases,
>and the further misery
>caused by the gap
>between the rich
>and the poor.
He asked of them first
a re-organization
of the whole of society
by chasing from it
the evil of that gap,
A society
in which there are
NO masters
and NO servants,
>a society
>in which all
>use their talents
>to the full
>in view of that society,

and in which all
receive all they need
without having to ask for it.
A society
in which the human family
is sitting around
ONE TABLE,
and there is
no
first one
and
no
second one
and
no
third one.
    A society
    in which the youngest,
    the child,
    is in the center
    of all human interest.
He did not ask them
to organize
a hospital-type of service
only,
        curing the effects
        of being underfed,
        kwashiorkor
        and tuberculosis;
        he asked them also
        and first
        to organize things
        in such a way
        that the evil spirit
        of irrational greed
        would be chased.
He did not ask them
to organize a clinic
only,

    healing venereal diseases,
    gonorrhea
    and syphilis;
    he asked them also
    to cast out
    that type of
    promiscuity
    that causes those
    evil ills.
First:
cast out;
second:
cure.
    He did not tell them only
    what to do.
    He told them too
    where to start.
    He said:
    "Do not go to Samaria,
    now;
    that will come later;
    do not go to
    non-Jewish countries;
    do not go to Greece,
    do not go to Rome."
        All sorts of biblical reasons
        are given by scholars
        to explain
        why he restricted himself
        and his disciples
        to his own people
        only.
There might be
a simple psychological reason.
We all have the tendency
to project evil
outside
our life and society.

When those disciples
heard
that they were going
to cast out evil spirits,
they, too, must have reasoned
like that:
>   the devil,
>   where is the devil?
>   not with us;
>   he is in Samaria,
>   he is in the Decapolis,
>   he is outside.
He told them:
"Start at home,
start among your own people:
>   they are in need,
>   they are harassed,
>   they are dejected,
>   they are oppressed,
>   they do not know
>   where to turn
>   next.
>   Start with them,
>   casting out
>   and curing."
But before Matthew's Gospel
ends,
those same twelve
are sent
"to all peoples
everywhere,"
and he added
that he would be
with them
to the ends
of the earth
and to the end
of the age,

casting out
evil and sin,
curing
their effects
also.

31.

IN THE PRESENCE
OF PEOPLE

Matthew 10:26-33

The Gospel of today
is rather mysterious.
It is about not being afraid;
it is about things that are
covered up
now,
but that will be in the open
tomorrow.
It is about the light
and the dark.
It is about rumors
and secret information.
It is about those who kill
and torture and imprison,
but who cannot kill the spirit.
It is about birds that fall
from the sky,
but that do not go unaccounted for.
It is about the registration
and the administration
of the number of our hairs
on our heads.

It is about all that,
but it all seems really to be about
how to witness to HIM,
JESUS CHRIST,
in this world
IN THE PRESENCE OF PEOPLE.
And he, Jesus, promises
that if we give witness
to him
in the presence of people
in this world,
that he then will witness
to us
with his Father
in heaven.
Sometimes I have the impression
that we Christians
do not take those sayings of his
seriously.
Sometimes I have the impression
that we are not willing to accept
his list of priorities.
We stick to our list,
and our list is different.
　　He said:
　　"Give witness to me in this world,"
　　he who healed,
　　　　and some Christians seem to draw
　　　　the conclusion that they only have to go
　　　　to church on Sunday,
　　　　to give a proof of their belief
　　　　in God.
　　He said:
　　"Give witness to me in the presence of people,"
　　he who fed the hungry,
　　　　and some Christians seem to draw
　　　　the conclusion that they only have to go
　　　　to prayer-meetings or
　　　　sermon-jam sessions.

He said:
"Love one another,"
    and some Christians seem to draw
    the conclusion
    that they only should stand up
    in charismatic meetings
    to witness and to contribute
    conspicuously to harambee*
    church building meetings;
        and they listen to the "epilogue"
        in the evening,
        and the "lift up your heart"
        in the morning,
        and the "daily service"
        every day.
*But is that the witnessing
he came to ask us for?*
Did he come asking us
to build churches
in honor of him?
        HE,
        who did not even want to own
        his own house in this world
        and who said very happily
        that he could not even call
        ONE stone his own
        in this world.
Did he come asking us
to build a temple
in honor of his Father?
        HE,
        who said to his disciples
        while they were admiring the temple
        at Jerusalem
        that he was going to destroy
        that temple,
        HE,
        who had answered
        that lady in Samaria

that God was no longer
to be worshipped
on mountaintops
or in temples,
but in spirit and truth.
Did he come to give us an opportunity
to organize church choirs,
or guitar-playing gospel-groups?
HE,
who told them
that those who only shout:
LORD, LORD,
will not enter the kingdom,
but that those will enter
who DO the will of his Father
over here
in this world
and he left no doubt
about that will.
He was not against praying;
he even told us how to pray.
He did NOT tell us
to call God
FATHER;
he told us
to call God
OUR FATHER.
First the word
OUR,
and only then the word
FATHER,
implying that we cannot reach
him
in our prayers
if we are not first willing
to relate to each other
as brothers and sisters,
as people with equal rights.

It is so easy to say Father
to God
and to forget
that OUR,
that family-of-God
spirit
he wanted.
Witnessing to Jesus
in the presence of people,
is witnessing
to that brother- and sister-hood.
He gave us a test.
When they asked him
where should we start,
he took in that world of ours,
in which one-third of the children are
sick and underfed,
a CHILD,
and he put that child
in the center of their circle
and he said:
"This is your test.
If you scandalize such a child
by refusing to take care of it,
God is not going to accept
you either."
He gave us a criterion.
On the last evening
of his earthly life
he said to his disciples:
"I am going,
but if you want to commemorate me,
if you want to witness to me
do this,
do as I do now."
And he took his bread,
he broke it
and handed it around,

and he took his cup,
and they all drank
themselves into the same
body.
> That is the witnessing
> he asks from us;
> in that test
> and in that criterion
> all is contained.
>> It is not the singing of
>> alleluia, alleluia, amen, amen,
>> that is going to save us
>> and this world.
>> That salvation is in
>> the breaking of the bread
>> and in the sharing of the cup.
>> In the breaking of MY bread
>> and in the sharing of MY cup,
>> and while doing that
>> we participate in the sacrifice
>> he brought to save us all,
>> and while doing that
>> we really should sing,
>> alleluia, alleluia, amen, amen.
>> We are saved through him.

*Harambee: going together. It is the national motto under the coat of arms of Kenya. A harambee meeting is a meeting where people come together to contribute to one or another project of public or private interest.

32.

WE NEED A CHURCH

John 21:15-19

You can do a lot about a church;
you can repaint it,
redivide it,
heighten it or lower it,
put in new windows,
floors, altars,
and statues.
  As long as you do not touch
  the pillars,
  really not very much
  happens
  to that church,
  with Jesus as the foundation
  and the cornerstone,
  with Peter and Paul
  as the pillars.
They are the pillars
not so much
structurally or
administratively,
but much more spiritually,
because they were the ones
who experienced Jesus
first,

and who understood
before so many others
how he, Jesus,
wanted us
to relate to God
and to him,
not alone,
not as individuals only,
not in a puritanical way,
but in a
community,
in the midst of brothers and sisters,
in a house,
in a family home,
where we are called together.
    Over here in this university,
    but also in other places,
    and situations,
    and times,
    religiously inclined people
        —I am not speaking
        about non-believers
        or atheists
        or nihilists—
    very often say:
    "I love God,
    I love Jesus,
    but I do not see the need
    for a church;
    I do not need others,
    I do not need structures,
    I do not need public prayers,
    confessions, communions,
    anointings, baptisms,
    and all those other things
    for that.
    I find God
        in my inner room,
        in my peace of mind,

in my personal relations,
in my corner,
in my Bible,
in my heart,
and in my soul.
He is nearer to me
than you
or you
or you."
People who talk like that
are sometimes very pious;
they don't even drink
a cup of cocoa
without saying grace;
they say prayers
day and night;
they live in a real
religious dimension,
but they are nevertheless,
according to Jesus,
wrong.
They are very simply
mistaken
or deceived.
Peter knew this;
it is the very heart
of the Gospel
of today.
That Gospel read:
"Peter, do you love me?
Do you love me,
personally?"
Peter's answer was:
"Yes, very much so;
you know that I love
YOU."
Jesus does not deny
that,
but he completes it:

"If that is true,
    take care of the others."
That was Peter's experience.
You cannot say: I love Jesus,
without loving your brother
and your sister,
without practicing that love
in the community,
that body and blood
called church.
        According to the Gospel
        it is impossible
        to relate to God,
            who remains
            invisible,
            silent,
            odorless,
            tasteless,
            and untouchable
            in *this* world,
        directly.
        It is only via and through
        our relations
        with others,
        it is only in our history
        together with them,
        that we can know
        about him.
At the moment
there are nevertheless
movements and orientations
that try to do
the opposite
among us religious
believers.
        The retreat houses,
        and prayer centers
        have been multiplying
        all over this world

to such an extent
that the United States
bishops' conference
even sent out a warning
that we have to be careful
not to build too many
heavenly escapes
in a world
in which we need
each other and
God
desperately.
Paul said the same thing in another
way.
He wrote the Corinthians
that he could not see
how they could celebrate Jesus
eucharistically
while some were hungry
and others overfed.

It is on that experience
of Peter and Paul
—that God,
and even Jesus Christ,
can be loved
only in a community
that cares—
that the church is built.
They are the pillars,
forever and ever
till kingdom comes.

33.

HIS BURDEN IS LIGHT

Matthew 11:25-30

Jesus speaks
about a yoke
in the text of today.
A yoke is a kind of stick
that you put over your shoulders
to carry a burden,
or better
to carry two burdens,
one on your right side
and one on your left side.
      But as hardly
      anybody uses a yoke
      anymore,
      it might be easier
      to stick to the second
      expression Jesus uses:
      burden.
And everybody knows
what a burden is.
All over the roads of this country,
Kenya,
people carry burdens,
food,
wood,

water,
and their belongings.
     Jesus says:
     "Take *my* burden,
     take the burden
     I want you to carry,
     because that burden is easy
     and light."
Jesus speaks about
"my yoke"
and
"my burden,"
suggesting
that there are other yokes
and other burdens
that we should,
according to him,
NOT carry.
     And he himself
     explained
     in the Gospel
     what those burdens
     are.
Jesus accused
the priests and the Pharisees,
the scribes and the "church"
of his time,
of having put burdens
on the people
that should not be there—
burdens that oppress.
     Did you know that
     according to their regulations,
     a Jew was not allowed
     to whisk a fly away
     that landed
     during a sabbath day
     on his nose or
     on his bald head?

He had to wait
until that fly
had finished its affairs
on that nose or
on that head,
whatever those affairs were,
and flew off.
Those regulations even
forbade Jesus
to take the lameness away
from a man
on the sabbath.
But Jesus said:
"Throw that burden away,
it is no good;
take my burden,
love."
Jesus accused
the political powers
of his time
of having put the burden of
submissiveness
on the people.
"You know"
   —and they all knew,
    as they all suffered
    under the colonial power—
"that your political leaders
rule over you,
calling themselves
your masters.
Throw that burden away,
that is not how it
should be
with you:
nobody should be a master
among you,
weighing on the shoulders
of others."

Jesus spoke not only
about yokes
and burdens
that others put
on our shoulders.
He spoke also
about the burdens
and the yokes
we ourselves put
on our own shoulders
on the shoulders of our
tired and terrorized
bodies.
> When that rich young man
> comes to him,
> stepping out of his brand new
> chariot,
> the latest model,
> or from his beautifully groomed
> horse,
> to ask him:
> "What should I do?"
> He looks at him,
> and he likes him
> at first sight,
> and he answers:
> "Take that burden of that wealth
> from your shoulders;
> sell everything
> you have,
> start another life,
> a new life;
> my burden is
> easy."
We carry so many
unnecessary burdens:
> we think that we should drive
> a very big,
> a very unhandy,

and a very petrol-consuming
car;
or when we are a small schoolboy,
we think we should have a watch,
even if we do not know
how to tell the time.
Do you know that small boy
Samson Mwangi,
who asked and asked and asked
in the morning,
in the afternoon,
in the evening,
and even during the night
in his dreams
for a watch?
And finally
he got one,
a beautiful one;
he put it on his wrist,
and he thought that he was
very happy,
and he showed his watch
to everybody.
But then he walked
through the street
with his big watch,
a very fancy one,
and a big boy
came to him
and he wanted to steal his watch
and he had to run,
and he did not dare
walk through the streets
with that watch
anymore.
He stayed at home.
Mwangi liked to play
football
very much,

but now
he could not play football
with that watch
anymore,
because he was afraid
that it might fall
on the ground:
what a burden that watch
became.
But even in other ways
things might become
a burden.
Advertisements force us,
burden us
        to eat a certain cereal
        at breakfast though it has
        the taste
        of overcooked old newspapers.
Advertisements force us,
burden us
        to buy very clumsy
        and very high,
        very dangerous,
        and very expensive
        platform shoes and
        all kinds of useless
        things like that.
They force on us the burden,
of being with it
        —with what?—
of being in
        —in what?—
        Some of us
        have our diaries full with
        appointments;
        others work late in the
        night;
        others again labor so much
        that they are never at home,

so that their own children
do not even recognize them
anymore
and ask during breakfast
when they see their own father
for once:
"Who is that man
over there?"
And Jesus says:
"Throw it off,
throw it away,
do not be burdened like that
    religiously,
    politically,
    consumerwise,
    and economically;
get free,
follow me!"
    And Saint Paul, in the second
    reading of today,
    wrote:
        "There is no necessity for us
        to obey our unspiritual selves;
        if you do that,
        if you burden yourself
        with all those things,
        you are going to be worried stiff,
        you are going to be overworked,
        you are going to end,
        you are going to die;
        put an end
        to all the strain
        you put on your body,
            eating wrongly,
            drinking wrongly,
            worrying wrongly,
            smoking wrongly,
            working wrongly.

Shake off those burdens;
BE MERCIFUL TO YOUR BODY
and you will live."
Jesus said:
"Take MY yoke,
carry MY burden;
it is light,
healthy,
and joyful."

34.

THE SEEDS OF
THE KINGDOM

Matthew 13:1-23

A man went out to
sow.
He must have had plenty of
seeds,
not twenty-two or thirty-six
of them
in a small envelope,
but bags
full.
    If you have a bit of seed,
    you dig a nice row of small holes
    and in each hole you put one seed
    or two;
    if you have plenty
    of seeds,
    you can go ahead
    over the field,
    and you throw the seeds out
    with wide
    and generous
    gestures.

Some fell in the field,
some fell on the rocks,
some fell on the tarmac road,
some fell in between thorny bushes,
and it all tried
to grow.
>Between the thorns
>it is strangled;
>on the tarmac road
>it has no way to push
>even the smallest of roots;
>on the rocks
>it dries up;
>but in the field
>it grows,
>two feet high,
>three feet high,
>ten feet high,
>enormous.
After this very simple story
his disciples came
to ask him
what he meant:
"Tell us";
and he explains.
>Today we have his explanation
>in Matthew;
>there is also an explanation
>in Mark
>and in Luke.
>Those explanations
>are different.
In Matthew
the seed is
"the message of the kingdom";
in Mark
the seed is
"the message of God";

and in Luke
the seed is
"the word of God."
> That word of God
> is not a word only;
> it is the sky,
> because he said:
> "Sky,"
> and there was the
> sky.

That word of God
is not talk only,
because he said:
"Light,"
and there was the
light.
> That word of God
> is not speech only,
> because he said:
> "Elephant,"
> and that big animal
> started to pound
> through the bush.

That word of God
is not mere chit-chat only,
because he said:
"Adam,"
and there he was
full of life;
and he said:
"Eve,"
and there she, too,
stood
splendidly
in the light
of the morning sun.
> That word of God
> is not a vibration
> of the air only,

because that WORD
became finally FLESH
in Jesus Christ.
When Matthew speaks
about *the message of the kingdom,*
he means that word
JESUS;
when Mark speaks
about *the message of God,*
he means that word
JESUS;
and when in Luke
Jesus says:
"The seed is *the word of God,*"
it is he himself.

    The sower
    is sowing his seed
    everywhere,
    generously,
    abundantly,
    hands-full of seed:
    the life of Jesus
    all over us,
    a gift from heaven
    just as all we have
    and all we are
    is a gift
    from God.
We are invited to receive
that seed
and let it grow
into fruits.
    It is in Jesus
    that the fullness
    and the liberty,
    the possibilities
    and the glory
    of human life
    are manifested.

The parable also tells
what can go wrong
with this gift
of life:
>   it can fall on tarmac,
>   on the smoothness
>   and the tightness
>   of the people
>   who do not want to live
>   or to get old,
>   who do not want
>   to mature and to get
>   wrinkles,
>   who do not want
>   to live at all.
It can fall
alongside the road
on the footpath,
where there are too many footsteps,
too much business,
and too much work,
where there is too much running
to be able to survive
and to enjoy
and to thank.
>   It can fall among the thorns
>   and be too over-stimulated,
>   over-excited, and
>   over-prickled
>   to be able
>   to live.
But that seed remains
in all circumstances
essentially
a gift from God,
a gift we should respect
not only in ourselves
but in others as well.

That life and that seed
is not only a gift that should
develop
in me,
because of myself,
but also because
of the others.
My life is not only
a gift
to me;
it is
God's gift to you as well,
just as your life
is not only a gift
to you,
but also
to me.
If all of us
would understand
and live
that reality,
the field of this,
our world,
would yield a crop
a hundred-,
a thousand-fold.

35.

WHEAT AND WEED

Matthew 13:24-43

I know a person
locked up,
isolated,
not speaking,
not helping,
not assisting,
because
all is wrong,
everything is rotten,
all goodness
is ambiguous,
all love mixed,
all spirit
dubious.
And I think
that all of us
have now and then
that same temptation
and frustration,
and that is why
for all of us who are
working at the kingdom to come
the Gospel reading of today
is very relevant.

The Gospel today
is again about that field
in which the seed
is growing up,
but all through that field
it is not only the seed
from the divine sower
that is growing up;
next to the wheat
there is a lot of
weed.
The Gospel today
tells us
that no one of us
is perfect;
that we, too,
are mixtures.
It tells us also
that we should not expect
anyone
to be perfect:
a wife cannot expect
her husband to be perfect;
to be only wheat
and no weed at all.
A husband cannot expect
his wife
to be without
tare.
If this is so
with all human beings
individually,
it is true as well
of all human structures,
organizations, and societies.
I don't think
that one social system
is as good
as another one.

There is a difference
between capitalism
and socialism.
But I am sure
that in both systems,
that in all systems,
the weeds will be found,
and they will never
disappear
totally
before the
end.
> They were even to be found
> in that so-called primitive
> Christian community
> that the Acts of the Apostles
> speaks about
> at the beginning of
> Christianity.
> They all lived
> together,
> they all prayed
> together,
> they all shared their bread
> together,
> they even shared the rest
> of their goods;
> but Ananias and Saphira
> kept something for themselves
> though they wanted to join:
> weed among the wheat.
The disciples
suggested to Jesus:
> "Let us tear out all imperfection,
> let us root up all those weeds,
> let us have a total revolution,
> let us have
> > a coup,

        a plot,
        an overthrow,
    let us have the kingdom
    NOW."
Jesus said:
    "Let it grow,
    let them grow,
    the wheat and the weed;
    if you try to separate them
    NOW,
    if you try to pull them all away
    NOW,
    all might get lost."
He did not say,
however,
that things
should remain
as they were;
he spoke about growth,
and about a final victory
of the wheat,
the good wheat
to be eaten
by all.
He suggests
in that way
that change
is possible.
        The wheat will
        overgrow the
        weeds.
        The power
        to change is in the
        divinely sown
        seed.
A drinker
can stop
drinking.

A mean man
can become
generous.
A lost person
can discover
meaning.
A smoker can
stop smoking.
> You can change your direction
> if you are sick and tired
> of the way you have been
> living.
> A narrow mind can
> expand.
> A racial bigot can make
> a friendly gesture.
> A thoughtless motorist can
> start controlling
> himself and his
> car.

We should not allow
the weed to overgrow the wheat.
We should try to be as little part
of the problem
as possible,
and to be as much part
of the solution
as feasible.
> But a mixture
> we will remain,
> until
> the last harvest is
> brought in.

36.

THE KINGDOM IS HUMAN LIFE

Matthew 13:44-52

That mysterious kingdom of his
must have always been
on his mind.
In the New Testament
there are almost 150 references
to that kingdom,
and the more Jesus speaks about it,
the more wrapped up in clouds
it seems to be.
    In the text of today
    he calls it:
        a hidden treasure,
        a box full of golden coins
        hidden somewhere in a field;
    he calls it:
        a precious pearl,
        a jewel found
        by a businessman
        who sells everything he has
        to buy it;

he calls it:
　　a fishing net
　　full of fish,
　　good ones and bad ones;
and before he had called it:
　　leaven and light,
　　salt and seed,
　　a ripe harvest,
　　a royal feast,
　　a great banquet,
　　an enormous party,
　　a wedding feast.
And all this is nice,
very nice,
but somewhere the question
remains:
what is that kingdom of God
here on earth?
　　Some think it is the actual world,
　　some think it still has to come,
　　some think it is heaven,
　　some think it is the ideal political order,
　　some think it is exclusively God's business
　　and that we have only to wait,
　　some think it is the church,
　　some even seem to think it is the town
　　Jerusalem.
What is that kingdom of God?
When did it start?
Where did it start?
How did it start?
　　In the beginning God divided the light from the dark.
　　Was the light the kingdom of God?
　　He then divided the land from the water.
　　Was the land the kingdom of God?
　　He then made the earth grow with weeds,
　　climbers and creepers, bushes and trees.

Were those plants the kingdom of God?
He made the seas and the oceans and the lakes
crawl with fish.
Were those fish the kingdom of God?
He covered the earth with animals of all kinds,
he filled the air and the sky
with insects and birds.
Were they the kingdom of God?
And then he made man,
and he made woman.
You and me.
And he took the face of that man,
and he took the face of that woman
in between his hands,
and he bent their faces backwards
and he blew
his spirit
in the noses
of those two,
and he said:
 "Live,
 you man
 and you woman,
 as I live.
 Rule over the world
 in such a way that you prosper;
 rule over the earth in such a way
 that you may be well and joyful,
 and give life,
 your life and my life
 to your children
 forever and ever."
That is the kingdom of God
here on earth:
HUMAN LIFE.
 God's kingdom is nothing else
 but God's will:

thy kingdom come,
thy will be done.
God's will is nothing else
but the well-being of people.
Nothing else.
That is one argument
to explain that the kingdom of God
here on earth
is human life.
There is a second proof.
The people around Jesus
recognized Jesus as the Son of God.
Why and how?
I think that they recognized him
as God's Son
because they discovered in him
that very same exclusive interest
in that divine issue:
the well-being of people.
Jesus always gave life.
He seemed in fact to be interested only
in that.
When he met a deaf man,
he said:
"Stop being deaf,
it is no good,
hear";
when he met a blind man
he said:
"Stop being blind,
it is no good,
see";
when he met a paralyzed person,
he said:
"Don't be lame,
it is no good,
jump";

when he met a speechless person,
he said:
"Don't be dumb,
it is no good,
speak";
when he met a bleeding woman,
he said:
"Stop bleeding,
it is no life,
get a child."
When he met that dead boy in Naim,
when he met that dead girl in Jairus's house,
when he met his dead friend Lazarus,
he said:
"Don't remain like that,
get out of your stupor,
live,"
and they all stood up
and danced with joy,
because of their life
regained, alleluia.
   He gave life,
   he restored life,
   he repaired life,
   he stimulated life,
   he tuned it up,
   he recommended it.
He did not do that
only in the physical
or bodily order.
He went also to people
who were spiritually blocked
or psychologically frustrated.
He identified himself
   with the poor,
   with the wretched,
   the prostitutes and adulterers,

the widows and the orphans,
the streetboys and the aged,
the crooks and the vagrants.
He unbound and loosened
Zaccheus,
—a very greedy and a very mean man,
a typical case of grabbiosis,
the grab-grab sickness—
so that that very mean man,
who thought only in terms of money,
changed completely
and became very generous,
as God is very generous.

God gave life
in the beginning,
good human life
everywhere.
And that is exactly
what Jesus did,
from the moment
he started,
and that is why they said:
"HE IS,
he must be,
THE SON OF GOD,
because he is interested only
in people's well-being,
the kingdom of God."

That was a second argument
to explain that the kingdom of God
here on earth
is human life.
There is a third one.

Last week,
over here in Nairobi,
representatives of all the bishops
of Africa met.

There were cardinals in red,
bishops in purple,
priests in black and white,
and all kinds of other colors.
They discussed the problems
of this continent Africa,
of their countries,
and of the world.
What did we Christians expect
from those leaders,
the representatives of Jesus Christ
here on earth?
Did we expect a new hymnal?
Of course not.
Did we expect a new liturgical dress?
No.
Did we expect an organizational
re-organization of the organization?
We did not.
We Christians expected from them,
because they are what they are,
statements
and, even more,
initiatives
on a greater human justice,
on a greater social equality,
on daily bread for all,
on the defense of human rights,
on the destruction of all weapons and war
that kill,
on a better family life,
on the plight of refugees
and on such *life* issues.
And we expect this,
because they should have
the interests of God and of Jesus Christ
at heart.

We expect this,
because they should foster
the kingdom of God
here on earth:
        a healthy human life
        for all,
        a greater attention for that
        only gift
        God really gave to humankind:
        LIFE.
But, brother and sister,
we should judge not only *them,*
those leaders,
on what they do and say,
or did not do and did not say
in the light of that kingdom of God
issue.
        We should judge ourselves too
        in that very same light:
        do we contribute in our work,
        in our decisions,
        in our education,
        and in all our activities
        to human well-being?
        Or are we like Zaccheus
        before he met Jesus,
        and before he started
        to live?
Let us invest in that kingdom of God.
It is the only investment that will last.
It is guaranteed by God himself,
who after the death and resurrection
of his Son Jesus Christ,
invested his own SPIRIT
in our
COMMON HUMAN LIFE.
Amen.

37.

HE TOOK THEIR BREAD AND FISH

Matthew 14:13-21

That morning
Jesus
got the news
that John the Baptist
had been killed.
I don't know
whether the news
was just that.
It might be that
the prison commander,
as so often happens,
had informed the public
officially,
that John the Baptist
had died in detention
because of a sickness;
or that he had committed,
unfortunately,
the official report added,
suicide,

he had suddenly lost his head,
      —that was true—
and had jumped out of the window
      —and that was a lie—.
    He had lost his head,
    he had been decapitated,
    he was dead,
    and hearing this
    Jesus wanted to be alone
    with his feelings,
    with his anger,
    with his consternation,
    with his fears,
    and with his disciples.
They took a boat
and went to a lonely place,
but the people,
who had heard of John's death
also,
started to follow him.
    In the context
    it is rather obvious
    that they went to him
    to ask for his reactions,
    that they went to him
    to ask what to do.
    He must have talked to them,
    unavoidably,
    on John.
        —What did people talk about
        the afternoon that President Kennedy
        was shot?
        —What did people talk about
        the evening that Martin Luther King
        was killed?
        —What did people talk about
        the day that Tom Mboya
        was murdered?*

—What did people talk about
the morning that James Kariuki
was found?†
    He must have been talking
    about John.
We do not know
what he said exactly;
we can only guess.
        He himself had told them
        that they were like sheep
        without a shepherd,
        and they asked him that afternoon,
        according to the report from John,
        to be their king.
        They asked him to take the lead,
        to be their guide,
        their shepherd,
        their king.
            He refused.
He must have been talking
about his kingdom in this world,
a kingdom that had been foretold
by that John the Baptist,
who had told his listeners
that someone was going to come
after him,
who was going to fill
THEM
with fire,
so that THEY would realize
the kingdom,
not only because others changed,
and were thrown over,
but because they themselves
had changed.
According to John's teaching
the kingdom had to come
from within us,

because of the Spirit
given to us.
> That kingdom cannot be introduced
> from the outside only;
> it has to grow
> from within.
> It has to grow from within us,
> because its frustration
> comes from within us
> too.

Why is alcoholism
so rampant
in this world?
Is it because people
like to drink?
Even if so,
why do they like to drink,
if not to overcome
the pain
in them,
> conscious or subconscious,
> their frustrations,
> their hunger,
> their feelings of incompetence
> or incapacity
> to educate their children
> and so on?

Why do people
drug themselves?
Why do they smoke
excessively?
Why do they masturbate
and fornicate?
Why do they sniff petrol,
or drink coffee
day and night?
Why do they steal and murder
and fight?

The other day
a social worker
came to talk
about a boy,
a child of twelve.
She said,
that boy is
no good.
He smokes opium,
he misbehaves.
But that boy
had been kicked out
by his mother
from her home
after his father
left her.
That boy is alone,
completely alone
at a time in life
that he needs his father
and his mother
so very much.
    Was his father bad?
    He was frustrated to death.
    Was his mother bad?
    She saw no means of survival
    together with the boy.
If such a boy
grows up
and has what we call "luck"
and makes it,
don't you think
that this in-built
lack of security
is going to make him
a very greedy,
a very grabbing
human individual?

Not because he is bad,
not because he is a monster,
but because he is sick
and has to be healed,
and nothing else
will be able to help him,
or us,
or this world.
Christ spoke that afternoon
about his kingdom,
in which human beings
should live
together
in another way,
        so that drugs,
        and greed,
        and war,
        and hunger
        do not exist
        anymore:
        a kingdom to come.
They got hungry.
The disciples wanted to send them
away.
But he said to them:
Why don't you give them
some food?
        And he took
        THEIR BREAD AND THEIR FISH,
        asking them to share,
        and healing them,
        then and there,
        with the fire
        of his Spirit.
And Saint Paul was so sure
that this kingdom
is going to come
that he wrote:

"Death nor life,
no angel,
no prince,
nothing that exists,
nothing still to come,
not any power
or height,
or depth,
nor any created thing,
can ever come
between us
and Jesus Christ,
the kingdom
to come."

* Tom Mboya was murdered in the center of Nairobi in 1969, most probably by political opponents of his ideas on African socialism.

†J. M. Kaviuki was murdered in 1973, most probably by his political opponents for his interest in the cause of the common person. His body was found near Nairobi on a path made and used by hyenas. He was found before those animals had a chance to eat his body.

38.

HE STEPPED OUT
OF HIS BOAT

Matthew 14:22-33

Today we have to commemorate
a pope,
Pope Paul VI,
who last week was still alive
and who is now
at this time
dead and buried,
in the same cave
as his predecessors,
together with Peter
the first pope.
    What Gospel reading
    do you take
    when you commemorate
    a pope like
    Paul VI?
A pope
    who liberated the liturgy
    out of its Latin prison
    in which it had been chained
    for centuries.

A pope
>who abolished the index,
>the list of forbidden books,
>and who left it to the Christians
>themselves to make out
>what they should read
>and what not.

A pope
>who decided to diminish the number
>of obligatory mortifications,
>abstinences and fasting,
>and who left it to the Christians
>themselves to determine
>how to commemorate
>the sufferings of Jesus Christ.

A pope
>who insisted again and again
>that we human beings should use
>our own consciences
>in all matters,
>marriage matters included.

A pope
>who unlocked the doors of his Vatican
>in which popes had been isolated
>for centuries
>and who went out,
>leaving Rome
>to visit the most far off places,
>geographically,
>economically,
>and religiously:
>he visited the slums of Bombay,
>and he wept;
>he visited the slums of Bogotá,
>and he wept;
>he was threatened with a brandishing knife
>by a deranged man in Manila,
>and he asked pardon for him;

he went to New York
to the United Nations
to plead for justice
and for peace
and for bread,
bread for all.
A pope
who came to Africa,
to this continent,
and he told the African church
to become itself.
A pope
who according to the experts
must have known that he was giving
Holy Communion
to people who were not Catholics,
to Hindus, Sikhs, and others
at the Eucharistic Congresses of
Bombay and Bogotá.
A pope
who said
that all people should be the artisans
of their own destinies,
that development is the new word
for peace.
What Gospel reading
do you take
when you commemorate
such a man?
I looked for a text,
and then I noticed the regular text
foreseen for this Sunday,
the nineteenth Sunday of the year,
and I could not find a better one
than the one foreseen officially
for today,
years and years ago
by a committee appointed by him.

It is the text you just heard;
it is the story
in which Jesus appears,
all light and shine,
walking over the troubled waters
and calling out to
the people in the boat of Peter,
tossed up by the wind and the storm:
"Come,"
and Peter,
the only one,
climbed out of his boat,
while the others stayed,
and Peter walked toward
him,
leaving the safety of the old rocking boat,
but as soon
as he was out,
and as soon as he felt
the force of the wind
and the power of the storm,
he took fright
and started to sink.
But Jesus said:
"Don't be afraid,
it is I."
And he put out his hand
and Peter held it.
Some years ago,
the lenten-letter of Pope Paul
was read
in this very chapel.
In that letter Paul
quoted an old Greek Saint,
Saint Basil,
who once wrote:
    that if anyone has two pairs of shoes,
    at a time that someone else has no shoes,

that second pair of shoes
does not belong
to the owner of those shoes
but to the one
who has none.
That second pair is not yours,
it is your brother's or sister's.
It was a theme Pope Paul VI
had also expressed
in his very famous encyclical
Populorum Progressio,
on the development of peoples.
He then wrote
(and he did not quote anyone else,
they were his very own words):
      "No one is qualified
      in keeping for his exclusive use
      what he does not need
      when others lack necessities."
And he then added
another quote,
this time from Saint Ambrose:
      "You are not making a gift
      of your possessions
      to a poor person;
      you are handing him over
      what is his."
That letter was read over here
in this chapel,
and that evening
rather late in the night
my phone rang,
and a rather threatening voice
asked me,
      who I thought I was
      to give such false
      and dangerous,

revolutionary and
subversive doctrine
in the name of the pope.
I answered
that it was the text
from the pope
and that this could be checked,
if necessary
at the Nunciature,
and the telephone call
was broken off.
        Not everybody wished
        to follow
        that man Pope Paul,
        who left his secure corner
        in the well-known boat.
Very often we speak of him
as the pope
who spoke so much
about sex,
on birth-control,
on celibacy,
and on things like that.
But if we remember him only
because of that,
then it is not because of him
or because of his hang-ups,
but it is because of ourselves
and because of our own hang-ups.
        All this can be seen,
        and should be seen,
        in the light of the real interests
        of this man Pope Paul,
        who had said at the end
        of the Second Vatican Council
        an amazing thing for a Pope,
        even for a liberated one.

He said:
"We are glad
that the Council has not only been
interested in the Church,
and in the Church's relations to God
and things like that,
because," he said:
"more than anyone else in this world,
are we interested in life,
in the cult
of human life."
He left his boat,
that secure and safe boat,
because of that interest
in human life;
he stepped into the storm
because of that concern,
just as his model
and inspiration,
Jesus Christ,
had left
his fatherly home.
    And a real suffering
    it was;
    he had his doubts,
    just like the Peter of the story
    of today.
    Once he had left the boat
    he sunk into
    very troubled waters.
In that same encyclical
on the progress of peoples
Pope Paul wrote:
    "Some might consider
    such hopes utopian."
        And he himself thought so
        most probably very often too.

He complained bitterly
about the lack of response,
he complained very often somberly
about his responsibilities,
He died like a rather old
and sad man,
and yet he himself had given
the answer
to his doubts,
when he continued:
"It might be that those persons
are not realistic enough
and that they have not perceived
the dynamism of the world,
which desires to live more fraternally,
a world,
which in spite of
    its ignorance,
    its mistakes,
    and even its sins,
    its relapses into barbarism,
    and its wandering from the road
    of salvation
is,
even unawares,
making sure steps
toward Jesus Christ,
over the sea
through the storm."
The glorified Christ
beckoned him out of his boat,
and he stepped out of it
into the troubled waters of this world,
    and we are invited
    to do the same.

39.

HE SAID NO

Matthew 15:21-28

Jesus said:
"No."
He refused
to heal.
The people around him
were amazed,
they were upset,
and,
if you read the story
carefully,
they were
angry.
They were looking at him,
who had said,
NO,
although the lady behind him
kept on shouting:
"Son of David,
have mercy on me,
Son of David,
help me!"
     He did not seem
     to be in a healing mood.

He had left his country
and his people
to be alone.
He wanted a rest,
a moment of peace,
and instead of helping him
in this,
his disciples kept on
asking him to perform.
HE had to perform
according to them,
all the time.
If he could do it,
why didn't he do it?
He refused,
but the woman
who had been shouting,
profited from their hesitation
and she came up to him
and she pleaded:
"Please,
Son of David,
help me."
She made a mistake
in that foreign,
non-Jewish country.
She appealed to him
as Son of David;
she appealed to him
as sent to the Jews;
she appealed to the God of Israel,
a God strange to her.
And Jesus used her mistake
to get out of the situation,
saying:
"Yes,
indeed,
I came for the Jews,

I am the son of David,
I did not come for you,
I came for Israel's children,
not for your child."
>   But she retorted
>   and said:
>   "I know you came
>   for those children.
>   But what about my child?
>   Are there no left-overs
>   at the table of the children
>   of the rich?
>   Help me,
>   give me a dog's scrap."
Jesus was struck,
but he stuck
to his
NO.
He did not change his opinion,
he did not go with her,
he did not touch the child,
he did not put any hand on her head,
he did not smear any of his spittle on her
demented forehead;
>   he told the woman:
>   you are of great faith,
>   you believe in my mission
>   among the Jews,
>   you believe in my power
>   among the non-Jews.
>   YOUR faith will help you.
>   What YOU want
>   will be done.
And her faith
healed her daughter
who had been possessed
by an evil spirit
for years and years.

Brother and sister,
preachers,
speakers,
leaders,
and pious people
very often talk
about that *faith*
that heals.
If you have faith,
they say,
then you can do
anything.
But what is that faith?
Is it belief in Jesus,
only?
Is it belief in God,
merely?
Do you remember
the first time
that Jesus
blames the Jews
for having no faith?
It happened in Nazareth.
He had explained himself.
He had spoken about
      the kingdom to come,
      justice to be established,
      a changeover to take place.
But they had murmured
among themselves:
      Where did he get those ideas?
      Isn't this the carpenter's son?
      Isn't this Mary's child?
      Isn't this the brother of James
      and Joseph?
      Don't we all know his sisters?
They did not believe in him,
nor in his divine possibilities,

because he was,
they grumbled,
like themselves.
        By not believing in him,
        and in his roots in God,
        they did not believe in themselves
        and in their roots in God.
They reasoned:
He is like us.
And who are we?
We are useless
and helpless.
        It was that reasoning,
        it was that belief
        that made them
        useless and
        helpless.
That is why they could not heal,
that is why they could not even
be healed.
        If they had believed in him,
        then they would have believed
        in themselves as well,
        as that woman did.
        She prevailed over him.
        She knew that he could not refuse
        if she referred to his mission,
        and it was HER faith
        that healed her child.
If we believed
in HIM.
then we would also believe
in OURSELVES.
If we believed in his power,
then we would believe in our power too
        and in our freedom too
        and in our responsibility
        and in our love

and in our hope
and in our forgiveness
and in God in us,
and our role
in life
would change,
and we would be healing
this world
day and night.

40.

THE ROCK UNDER
THE KINGDOM

Matthew 16:13-20

Jesus had been with them
for quite some time.
They knew about his baptism
and about what had happened
at that moment.
They knew about his temptations,
how he was tempted to be like
all the others:
    possession-hungry,
    honor-hungry,
    and power-hungry.
They knew how he had
refused.
    They knew about his healings;
    they had heard his sermon on the mount,
    and his teaching
      on human happiness,
      on the law,
      on anger,
      on marriage,
      on revenge,

on enemies,
on charity,
on prayer,
on fasting,
on wealth,
and on practically
all other aspects of
human life.
They had heard his parables
on the kingdom of heaven,
and they had seen with their own eyes
how that kingdom
was not only
a dream,
a string of words,
a set of ideas,
a utopia,
an illusion,
or hope.
They had seen that kingdom
realized in him.
They had seen him
as a total master
over nature and chaos;
they had seen him walking over
the water of the lake,
and they had seen Peter,
just for a moment,
participating
in that mastership,
by believing too.
They had seen him
multiply the bread;
they had seen in him
a human being
relating
in a divine way
to all forms of human life:

the young and the old,
the healthy and the sick,
the rich and the poor,
the just and the lost,
the Jew and the non-Jew.
They had seen in him
a human being
as no one had ever
seen before.
And now he came
to ask them:
"Who do you say I am?
What do you think of me?
What do you think of my style?
What do you think of my life?
What do you think of the Son of man?"
And nobody said a thing,
nobody dared to say anything,
nobody dared to evaluate.
Nobody wanted to deny
the validity of his life
and his person;
but nobody wanted to confirm
its validity either,
because that would mean:
to change your own
life.
Until Simon spoke up
and said:
"You know who you are.
I will tell you,
who I think you are:
you are the Messiah,
you are the son of the living God,
you are it,
you are what a human being
should be;
that is who you are."

And then Jesus spoke out,
and he said to Simon:
    "You see this
    because my Father made you see this;
    you know this
    because my Father made you know this;
    you feel this
    because my Father made you feel this;
    you believe this
    because my Father helped you believe this;
    and that is why you,
    Simon,
    are going to be the leader,
    a man of rock.
    It is on your type of faith
    and belief
    that I will build my community,
    my church,
    my salvation
    to the world."
It was within the context
of that belief in Jesus
and in his kingdom
that Peter got
his authority.
That belief is his authority.
It was because of that vision
that Peter got his
power.
    Not a power over persons,
    not the power to open or close
    heaven,
    as we tell our children;
    but the power
    to recommend and to forbid,
    the power
    to give guidelines
    and instructions,

so that the kingdom
he saw
will be realized
in this world.
The gospel text of today
is a very important one.
Up to this episode
Jesus had been alone.
He did what nobody else
had ever done;
he lived as nobody else
had ever lived.
But after this episode,
he had been recognized officially,
he had been understood by Peter,
and the others had agreed.
That recognition meant
for them:
a changeover,
a conversion,
new life.
For us
too.

41.

SAVING ONE'S LIFE

Matthew 16:21-27

Jesus had called Simon
Peter,
rock,
foundation
and key to the kingdom,
because it was
Peter
who had received
sufficient vision
from the Father
to be able to confess:
"You are the Christ,
the son of the living God."
    That confession,
    that affirmation
    made him the leader,
    and that avowal
    and acknowledgment
    changed his life
    from old
    to new.
But when Jesus
says,

as he does in the text of today,
that the newness
he brings
also means death
to the old ways
and a loosening
of the old ties,
Peter says:
> "No,
> not that.
> We do want the new way
> but not at the cost of
> the old way.
> We do want a new life
> but not at the cost of our
> old life.
> We want to be a branch
> grafted on you,
> the new vine,
> but we do not want to be cut
> away from the old tree.
> We do want to bring forth fruits,
> but we do not want to die
> first
> in the earth."

Jesus looks to him.
Jesus is,
as he himself admits,
tempted to listen to him,
but he does not listen;
he overcomes
the temptation
again
and he turns
against Peter
and hisses:
> "Get away, Satan,
> get behind me;

you are an obstacle.
I called you rock,
and now you are
a stumbling-block,
a stumbling-stone,
an obstacle."
And he *then* continues
saying:
"If you want
to follow me,
you have to renounce yourselves
as you are now;
you have to lose the life
you are living now;
and if you are not willing
to do that,
if you want to keep the life
you are living now,
then there will be no newness,
no vision
possible for you.
My vision
means passion."
Brother and sister,
there are so many followers
of Jesus Christ
in this world;
the Catholic ones alone
count 700,000,000.
More than one-third of humankind
is Christian.
Their vision
definitely
changed
the world;
there is no doubt
about that
and yet:

Why are things
growing so slowly?
Why is so much money spent
on the defense
of an old type of lifestyle,
while so many others
are starving
and, maybe still worse,
thirsting?
Is it not
because too many of the
followers of Jesus Christ
want at the same time
to have their cake
and to eat it?
Is it not
because too many Christians
are willing to cooperate
in the establishment
of the kingdom of heaven,
while sticking at the same time
to the kingdom of this world?
You cannot live
the old way of life
and contribute
to the new type of life
really.
You cannot overcome
the old order,
the hunger, the sin,
and the injustices
by giving alms
without dying to the
old way of things.
Christ said:
"Come on,
carry my cross,
help me carry it.

The grain of wheat
 must die
to
flower
and grow
into seed
a hundredfold."

42.

COMMUNITY DYNAMICS

Matthew 18:15-20

He gave them their leader,
the rock.
He set their way,
to die to the old
and to march
into the new
community.
>The newness had been formed,
>the ideal was set.
>Difficulties
>had to be foreseen.
>The new life invaded
>an old one;
>the kingdom had started,
>but it
>had not yet won.
>A brother could go wrong,
>a sister could fail.
What do you do
in such a case?
What do we normally
do
in such a case?

We see another
about him,
we talk to another
about her,
until all who matter
know,
except the one
who is failing.
Things get worse,
nobody assists,
everybody mocks,
everybody waits,
everybody watches,
and after the final
disaster,
we poor and petty
prophets
parody
that gift from God,
and we say
triumphantly:
          "Didn't I tell you!
          Exactly as
          I foresaw!"
And proud of our
life-experience,
we leave the victim
alongside the road,
where we knew
that he
or she
would slip,
and we
gloat.
          Those are not his rules.
          That is not his law.
          His community-dynamics
          are different.

Rule one:

  If your brother or sister
  does something wrong,
  don't leave her alone,
  don't leave him alone;
  go to him,
  or go to her
  and have it out
  in the open
    —not with their brothers
    or sisters,
    friends or
    enemies,
    but with them.

Rule two:

  If they listen,
  they are won back.
  If they don't listen,
  take another one
  with you,
  or even two.

Rule three:

  If they do not listen
  to those
  bring them into the
  community,
  and if that does not
  help,

Rule four:

  treat them as still
  belonging to the old
  before-the-kingdom-of-heaven
  order.
  And I,
  God,
  will abide
  with your
  decision.

> That seems hard;
> there is the possibility of
> a final,
> by-God-confirmed
> condemnation or
> excommunication.
> But that is not
> true,
> because God,
> our God,
> was going to bind himself
> to another rule,

Rule five:

> if two or three,
>> —the ones visiting
>> that brother and sister
>> included—
> agree to ask
> anything at all,
> it will be granted
> to them
> by my Father in heaven.
> And how would that brother
> or sister
> be able to resist
> that grace?

43.

RESTORATIVE POWER

Matthew 18:21-35

The question was:
"How often must
I forgive my brother
who wrongs me?"
 The answer was:
 "How often would you,
 yourself,
 need forgiveness
 from him?"
And in the story
that answer is strengthened
by indicating
that WE owe much more
to another,
than the others owe
to us.
 There is even
 a proportion given.
 It is
  —according to reliable
  experts
  on the economy
  of that time—

something like US $1,000,000,000
against about US $100.
The point of the story
is not only
that we should forgive,
or how we should forgive,
but also
that
we are able to forgive!
When we speak about the gifts
of God,
or about the gifts
of the Holy Spirit,
we very often think
immediately,
about
the light and
the fireworks
of Pentecost:
the fire,
the noise,
the thousands
in the street,
the storm,
the gift of tongues,
the gift of foreign languages,
the prophecy
and its interpretation,
the laying on of hands,
the healings,
the evil spirits
sprinting away,
the streams of baptismal
water,
and all the conversions.
And we overlook
that other time
when very calmly

—and wasn't God
to be found in
the gentle breeze
of the Old Testament
and not in its
storms?—
Jesus blew
over them
and said:
    "You can forgive,
    I give you the power
    to forgive.
    You *can* absolve,
    you *can* forgive
    and you *can* set free."
If there is one gift
of God
we need
in our days
it is that gift
of forgiveness.
It is only
over the bridges
of forgetting forgiveness
that humankind,
        the Africans and
        the Europeans;
        the Indians and
        the Chinese;
        the Jews and
        the Arabs;
        the Americans and
        the Russians;
        the exploiters and
        the exploited;
        the plunderers and
        the plundered;

the old and
the young;
the fighting brothers and
the fighting sisters,
can be brought together
in Jesus,
who died
for all,
in view of a kingdom
that will come
to its fullness
at the moment
that we all
forgive,
follow him,
and forget.

44.

ROYAL SYNCHRONIZATION

Matthew 20:1-16

The kingdom of heaven
is like a landowner
who hired his men
     in the morning,
     during the morning-break,
     at midday,
     during the afternoon-break,
     and an hour before all work
     stopped.
He promised the ones
he hired in the morning
the normal pay
for a day's work
     —in that time about
     fifteen cents.
He did not promise
the others anything
specific,
but they must have thought
that he would work
with the same
scale.

They were employed
with almost twelve hours
difference.
Some suffered
the heat of the day;
some had found hardly the time
to report
on their job.
They all got the same
full-day
pay,
the last ones first
and the first ones last.
It is those last ones
who started to complain.
They did not complain
about their fellow workmen;
they had no grudge against
their colleagues.
They complained
about their employer,
that landowner,
that king,
who had pulled them
all together
timewise.
Any social worker
or charitable volunteer
must have had
the same type
of experience.
You give a blanket
to one refugee,
and all the others come
to claim their blanket
too,
by right.

You give a pair of shorts
to one orphaned streetboy,
and they all come
to get,
they say,
"What is ours."
     His kingdom
     does not work
     like that.
     Its whole reality
     is a gift.
     Nothing can be
     claimed.
     Creation comes
     from nothing,
     point zero.
Right and just
fall away
against the force
that put it into
being:
God's love,
God's sharing love.
     We have no ground
     to stand on
     other than that
     one.
     We have no time
     to live in
     other than God's one.
It is God
who chooses,
it is God
who synchronizes all
in his
eternal
instant
NOW.

45.

TO PRAY IS NOT ENOUGH

Matthew 21:28-32

There are those two sons,
two sons of God
the Father.
They both believe,
they are both willing to listen,
they are both open to him.
    That is why the Father
    speaks to them.
    He tells them both:
    "Go,
    and work
    in my world!"
Number one is very obedient
about it.
He answers:
    "Yes, Father;
    of course, Father;
    okay, Father;
    as you wish, Father;
    no problem, Father,"
but he disappears
and does not care
at all.

He answered
beautifully,
very piously,
very serenely,
and very solemnly.
He crossed himself
twice,
he bowed his head
before he left,
and at the door,
he turned around
once more,
he even sprinkled himself
with some water.
But he went away
to do nothing.
The Father
spoke also
to his second son.
He too listened,
but he said
very clearly:
"I am sorry,
but my answer
is NO.
I am too busy myself,
I have no time
to worry
about
your world;
bye, bye."
And he too
left.
He did not bow
his head;
he did not show any
further respect;
he did not cross himself
even once;

he did not turn around
at the door
anymore.
He left,
but once
in the world
he did
what his Father
had asked him to do.
     The question is obvious:
     "Who did the Father's will?"
     The answer too:
     "The second one."
Both brothers had been
in contact with their Father.
Both had listened.
Both had prayed,
both responded.
But for the first one,
his words remained words.
The words of his Father
and the words he spoke
himself.
The second one
stepped out of his words,
and he started to work
taking up
his responsibility
in his Father's world.
     So many believers
     seem to be believers
     in words only.
     The church is their favorite
     place,
     to make up their minds
     to do nothing
     when the Father calls.
     They are overeager to
     recite:

Father, Father,
Lord, Lord,
Jesus, Jesus,
Amen, Amen,
alleluia, alleluia.
They visit
chapels,
churches,
temples, and
shrines.
They say
morning-prayers,
evening-prayers,
prayers before and after
meals.
Their words sound like:
yes,
yes,
But their attitude
is
NO, NO.
We will be judged,
not on what we say,
but on what we do;
not on how we relate
to the Father
in words;
but on how we relate
to his world
in deeds.
Our temple is
this world
till kingdom
comes.

46.

DELIVERING THE GOODS

Matthew 21:33-43

Some time ago
a student came to my office.
He knocked rather cautiously
on the door,
and he entered rather strangely.
He opened the door,
closed it quickly,
looked around
even before he looked at me,
looked once more back at the door,
tried whether he had closed it well,
and then he sat down,
while I had the impression
that he tried to look
at the same time
under my desk
to see if something
had been hidden
under there.
He looked like a persecuted man,
he looked as if
a danger
was following him.

259

He finally settled down,
looked once more around,
and said:
"I need your advice;
I don't like this place,
I want to go."
I asked him why.
He answered:
"Those people over here
at the university
are dangerous.
They not only teach
how things are;
they teach also
how they should be;
and that is what I don't like.
It is too dangerous,
I am leaving."
If you buy the *Sunday Nation*
of today
you can read an interview
by John Esibi
of the vice-chancellor of this university.
And in that interview Dr. Karanja
criticizes the staff.
He does not do that directly,
but indirectly,
by stating
that the staff is free
to try
to right society's ills:
that they should communicate
their knowledge,
that they have to be relevant
to national development,
that they have to be vocal
as a constructive minority.

It is as if he suggests
that, though working,
they do not render
the fruits expected.
That is what the Gospel text of today
is about.
It is about another group of people,
who were put in God's world,
in his *shamba,**
to get all they could out of that
land,
and who remained fruitless.
They not only remained fruitless,
they were even reactionary.
They not only refused to cooperate,
they aggressively rejected
a change,
and all the prophets
that came to ask them
to change their society
were killed by them,
even
when
God
decided
to send
his son
Jesus.
    What did that Jesus want?
    It might seem difficult
    to describe
    what he wanted
    precisely.
    He did not give many
    economic
    sociological,
    or political indications.

He gave only some principles,
and his main principle
seems to have been
the
"God-is-our-Father" principle
and the connected
"we-are-therefore-brothers-and-sisters"
working theory.
Next to that
he made it clear
that this "Father-principle"
will work only
if all people
are capable
of living their human lives
to the full,
and that the world should be organized
in such a way
that all people can develop
totally
the talents
given to them by God.
While he worked with this message
among his contemporaries
he insisted that those principles
were overlooked
neglected and even contradicted
by the religious leaders,
by the rich,
by the political leaders,
but also by practically every
individual.
He stressed the point
that things should change,
not all of a sudden
in one terrific, bloody
revolution,
but slowly.

That is why he spoke
about a SEED
that he sowed in the field
and that was going to grow.
He spoke about
a vineyard,
about growth,
about waiting
and tending.
        In the responsorial psalm
        we read today
        three times
        that that vineyard
        (and the seed)
        is the house of Israel.
That is true,
and it is not true.
It was true
in the time of Jesus.
For us
the vineyard
(and the seed)
is Kenya,
and the farmers
are *we*.
        Jesus presents himself
        to us
        over here.
        We can take him,
        we can leave him.
        Brothers and sisters,
        let us take him
        and render the fruits,
        delivering the goods.

*Shamba: Swahili for field.

47.

IT SHOULD BE A FEAST

Matthew 22:1-14

The kingdom of heaven
may,
according to the Gospel,
be compared
to a feast,
to a party,
to a never-ending treat,
to a festival,
    —and let us not forget
    that according to Jesus
    that kingdom starts
    already here
    on earth.
This description
differs
from what Christ's preachers
often make us believe.
If you listen to them
over here in the streets of Nairobi
that feast seems very far off,
if they preach it
at all.

They preach
that we are sinners
turning around
in the mud and the dirt
of sin
and spoiled human relations.
They preach
that we should convert,
and very fast too,
because the unavoidable end
is coming.
They preach about that end
in fire and sulphur,
blue smoke and very hot flames,
with devils poking
at our ribs.
>They speak very much
>about that conversion,
>but it does not seem
>that human life
>will get better
>after that hoped for
>turnabout.
>What do you do
>after that conversion:
>>pray?
>>sing alleluia?
>>drink water?
>>eat bread?
>>remain unmarried?
They are the prophets of doom,
like John the Baptist,
and like that other prophet
Jonah,
who walked three days
through the town of Nineveh
saying:

doom,
disaster,
death,
destruction,
disintegration,
hell,
the end,
and who,
in a way,
even seems to have liked
that terrible
mission.
Those prophets
are not complétely
wrong.
We are sinners,
we should convert.
If we do not change over
things will get worse
and finally collapse
or explode.
But they are incomplete
and therefore
wrong also.
We are in first
and in last instance
invited to a feast.
We are created
and saved
to celebrate our human life
here on earth
and in all time
to come.
Very many Christians
lost that idea;
they think that we are born
to suffer
over here,

and most probably also
over there.
It is not true,
it cannot be true,
and African Christians
have known this
from the very beginning.
In 1846
Johan Ludwig Krapf
and Johan Rebman
opened, over 130 years ago,
the first Christian church
of modern times
in what is now called Kenya,
at Rabai,
fifteen miles inland from Mombasa.
They invited the Warabai
to the opening of that church.
Fifteen men came.
They sung a hymn,
there was a Gospel reading
in Kiswahili,
another hymn,
one of those slow ones,
one of those sad ones,
a prayer,
a long sermon,
another hymn,
and the service
was over.
Krapf hurried
after the service
to the door
to meet the people
coming from church.
He asked them:
"How was it,
are you coming back?"

They looked at him
and said:
"No."
He asked them:
"Why not?"
They answered:
"We do not pray
as you do.
There should have been
rice,
a bullock should have been
butchered,
there should have been
beer;
that is how we pray to God;
it is a feast."
Krapf said:
"You are
sinners."
They asked him
what he meant,
and Krapf explained
what sin was,
and why they were
sinners.
They said:
"Who told you
those stories
about us,
who has been defaming us,
who has been gossipping,
who has been backbiting?"
Krapf said:
"But God loved you so much
that he sent you
his only son;
that is the proof
of his love."

One elder then
said:
"Of course, God loves us;
he sends us his rain.
he sends us beer,
and our clothes
and our children—"
implying that he did not need
Jesus
to know all this.
    I do not say
    that we are not sinners.
    I do not say
    that we do not need conversion.
    I do say,
    that Jesus Christ
    came to invite us
    to a celebration
    of the real gift we got
    from our Father in heaven,
    our human life.
We should celebrate that life,
enjoy it,
    bodily,
    spiritually,
    psychologically,
    fully.
And if you ask me then,
and what about *sin?*
    Sin is sin,
    because it hinders
    and blocks that celebration:
    that is why murder is sin,
    that is why envy is sin,
    that is why hatred is sin,
    that is why theft is sin,
    that is why apartheid is sin,
    that is why injustice is sin,

that is why exploitation is sin,
that is why loose human relationships are sin,
that is why war is sin,
that is why neglecting your children is sin,
that is why corruption is sin.
We should convert,
but not with that nagging idea
in our head
that after our conversion
everything is as dull
as an empty churchbuilding
on an afternoon
during the week,
or even as dull
as a hymn-singing congregation
on a rainy Sunday morning
in a dark and cold church.
    After our conversion
    life should start to be
    a feast.
    Christ started his ministry
    at Cana.
    He gave them seventy-two cases
    of beer.
    He ended in Jerusalem
    where he gave them
    his last supper,
    his bread and his wine,
    his body and his spirit,
    and he did not stop saying:
        "I came to bring
        you
        LIFE.
        Take it up
        and really enjoy it.
        The more you enjoy it,
        the surer I am
        of your thankfulness."

48.

A TAX THAT IS
NOT YET PAID

Matthew 22:15-21

Some Pharisees and some Herodians
came to ask Jesus a question.
At least that is what they pretended
to do.
They came to ask him a very good question,
in fact it is one of those burning issues
that has been worrying
very many Christians and very many others
all through human history:
      should one pay tax
      to a political organization
      that is unjust,
      that exploits,
      that oppresses,
      and that has no respect
      for human rights?
It was a good question
in Jesus' time
when the Romans
were exploiting
the Jews,

271

but it is still
a good question
for any Christian
living in South Africa,
where tax money is spent
to subdue and frustrate
the larger part of the population.
It is a good question in Rhodesia,
but it is also a good question
in those countries
where it has been decided
to spend tax money
on the development of nerve-gases
and on the improvement
of atomic warheads
and on all kinds of
anti-human-life
and *therefore*
anti-kingdom-of-heaven
devices.
It is with that question
that those Pharisees
came to Jesus.
They did not come,
however,
because they were interested
in his answer.
They had the answer
already in their pockets,
because they carried with them
the coins
a Jew had to buy
to be able to pay
tax,
coins with the head of the emperor
on them.
They did not come for an answer
at all.

They came to trap him.
If he said:
"No,
you should not pay,"
he would be caught by the Roman
police.
If he said:
"Yes,
you should pay,"
he would be caught by his
people
as a collaborator.
They wanted to catch him,
as they did afterwards,
when they shouted from behind his back:
"Condemn him,
crucify him,
he told us
not to pay
your tax."
They did not come for an answer
at all.
They had not listened
to any of his answers
up to then.
They had asked him:
"What should we do?"
And he had told them:
"Sell all you have,
give it to the poor,
and be like me";
they had only laughed,
walking away.

    They did not come for an answer,
    in order to liberate with him
    the poor and the oppressed.
    They themselves were oppressors
    of those poor.

It is Jesus himself
who had accused them,
those Pharisees and other religious leaders,
that they despised the poor,
that they looked down upon them,
and that they had laid on the shoulders
of those poor
extra burdens they themselves
were not willing to carry,
but from which they profited
scandalously.
That is why he told them:
"Hypocrites,
you only came to set me
a trap.
You do not care a fig,
but I will give you
my answer;
show me one of those coins."
And one of them
was naive enough
to do just that;
he put his hand in his pocket
and produced one.

He took the coin,
he tossed it head-side up
and asked:
"Whose face is that?"
He was answered:
"It is the emperor's head."
And he threw the coin back
and said:
"If that is the emperor's face,
give to the emperor,
what is of that emperor,"
and he then added
his real answer,
an all over-ruling answer:

"and give to God
what is God's;
give to God
what carries God's face;
give to God
what is created
in God's image."
With that answer
a whole new world opened up:
What is created in God's image?
What is imprinted with God's face?
What does God expect us
to give him?
  Not a church,
  not a pile of bricks,
  not blocks of cement,
  nor pieces of gold and silver,
  nor all kinds of prayers,
  nor the tickling of guitars,
  nor the nice songs of competing choirs,
  not even four Our Fathers,
  or signs of the cross,
  or endless Hail Marys.
    All that is good,
    all that can help,
    but what he wants us to give him
    is a well organized
    HUMAN LIFE
    for all.
That is the worship he wants,
that is the tax
we have to pay
to belong
to his kingdom
here on earth.
    As long as there are in this world
    starving children
    and refugees,

sick people that are not helped
and poor who have no means
of being educated,
and rumors of war,
pest, plague,
etcetera,
we should not rest:
    our worship is not complete,
    we did not render to God
    what he wants us to render to him:
    a fully developed human life
    for all.
    Our tax to him
    is not yet
    paid.

49.

WHY DOES OUR LOVE NOT WORK?

Matthew 22:34-40

We should love God
with all our heart,
with all our mind,
with all our soul,
and our neighbors
as ourselves.
We all know this
and we have known it
for ages.
        Yet,
        2000 years after
        the death of Jesus Christ
        the successors of his apostles
        in 1970 came
        together in Rome
        to state:
        "In the face of the present-day
        world situation,
        marked by the grave sin of injustice,
        we recognize our responsibility
        and our inability to overcome it
        by our own strength."

277

We really do not need
those bishops
in their synod
to know this.
        Over the last week
        we had over here on the campus
        two meetings
        in our Catholic community context
        where the same remarks
        were made.
There was a meeting
on the neglected streetboys
of Nairobi,
with beautiful slides
on this great problem
and the solutions proposed,
but then one of us said
        —and I hope he does not mind
        being quoted—
"What we do is just
like raking leaves
from under a tree.
Next day there will be
other leaves.
If we want to do something
definite
that tree has to be rooted up;
but we can't do that!"
        And in another meeting
        on "Youth, Freedom, and Love,"
        another student
            —and I hope she does not mind
            being quoted—
        remarked:
        "It is very nice to listen
        to this type of talk
        and to listen to all the sermons
        in the chapel,

but every time that I decided
to do something,
I did not know
what to do,
or where to start.
It all seems to be
an exercise in frustration."
Those bishops said:
we recognize our responsibility,
and our *inability.*
They spoke as leaders
of what we might call
organized religion,
an organized religion
that has been preaching for so
long
that we should love each other
as we love ourselves,
and it never seems to have
worked.
That is true;
organized religion
does not seem
to work.
    In April 1977
    the American journal,
    U.S. News and World Report,
    made a research report
    to rate institutions, organizations,
    and activities
    in regard to their influence
    on
    "decisions or actions affecting
    the nation as a whole."
In that research
organized religion
came out as
number 26!

Why is that?
Why do we as believers
in the power of God
in us
have less influence than
   the government,
   television,
   trade unions,
   the court of law,
   big business,
   the Senate,
   state bureaucracy,
   banks,
   newspapers,
   political parties,
   the family,
   the legal profession,
   radio,
   advertisements,
   magazines,
   and so on?
Why?
I think it is
because we are
not sufficiently
profiting
from what others
discovered long ago.
Our religion and
our love
are too old fashioned.
   We do love as individuals,
   we do love within our small groups,
   but we do not participate
   lovingly enough
   at a societal level.
Sigmund Freud,
the famous psychologist,

healed at first
by treating individuals only;
he then discovered the possibilities
of group therapy.
But at the end of his life,
just before his death,
he spoke about the need
for research
in the pathology
of modern community
as such.
　　　We can love at different levels;
　　　we can love
　　　as a child,
　　　concentrated on
　　　oneself.
We can love
as an adolescent,
concentrating on
some interpersonal relations.
　　　We can love
　　　as an adult,
　　　participating
　　　in human history
　　　at the level of
　　　human community.
It might be there
that organized religion fails.
That might be the reason
that we as Christians
very often feel
frustrated.
　　　We should have
　　　the same interests as God;
　　　we should be suffering
　　　as he does,
　　　according to the first reading
　　　from the book of Exodus today:

"If you take another's cloak
as a pledge,
you must give it back to him
before sunset.
It is all the covering he has;
it is the cloak he wraps his body in;
what else would he sleep in?
If he cries to me,
I will listen,
for I am full of pity."
We should be interested
in the individuals
    —Jesus transformed them
    calling them—;
we should be interested
in good personal relationships
in our families and in a community
like this one
    —Jesus healed those relationships
    and he built that type of community;
    it is he too,
    who built this one—;
we should be interested
in transforming the whole of society
    —as Jesus tackled
    the injustices and oppressions,
    the *sins*
    of his time
    and age—
together with
HIM.

50.

SOCIETY AS HE SAW IT

Matthew 23:1-12

Some time ago
two persons appeared
before a police officer
at Central Police Station.
One was a student,
the other one a messenger
of the university.
They had been arrested together.
    The officer asked the first one:
    "Who are you?
    What are you doing in life?"
    He gave his name and
    he said:
    "I am a second-year student
    at the University of Nairobi."
The officer asked the second one:
"Who are you?
What are you doing?"
He gave his name and
he said:
"I am a messenger
at the University of Nairobi."

The policeman
got very angry,
and he shouted
at the student:
"How is it
that we arrested both of you
together?
How is it
that you, a student,
were in the company
of that low-class scum,
a messenger?"
And it was on that point
that the constable
disagreed
with the Gospel text
of today.
    Nobody should be called master,
    because you are all brothers and sisters.
    Nobody should be called father
    because you are all children
    of the same Father.
    Nobody should be called teacher
    because you are all learners
    of the same teacher, Jesus.
He does not say
that all people are equal,
in the sense that we do not have different
    functions,
    gifts, or
    talents.
He admits that very candidly
in the same text of today.
He says of the scribes and the Pharisees
that they are sitting
on the chair of Moses,
and that is quite something.

He even says
that the others have to listen
to what they say
from that chair.
He has no difficulties
with their function
of spiritual and other leadership,
but he cannot stand
the way they behave
because of that function.
They made themselves
different from the others.
They walked around
better dressed
with all kinds of indications
of their self-invented
rank and order.
They wore beautiful sashes,
they had ribbons all over their chests
and foreheads.
They wanted to sit in front,
and they did not converse with those people
they called,
full of contempt,
the *"wananchi,"*
the "men of the street."
They wanted to be respected
and to be greeted;
they insisted on their
titles
and in all those ways
they discriminated,
they divided,
they cut up
that ONE human family
as willed
by God.

They were undivine,
they sowed hatred,
they wanted to shine
and to appear on the front pages.
They used their elbows all the time,
they oppressed
and they exploited.
We should not be
like them.
        In 1973 in Alwar, India,
        on the seventh of July,
        a bus was washed away
        from a road
        by a flood.
        Seventy-eight people drowned,
        only eight were saved.
The passengers
belonged to two different
high-caste communities
and they refused
to share
the ONE rope
that might have helped
all of them
to safety.
        We might laugh
        at such an example.
        We might laugh
        at the police officer
        in the beginning of this sermon;
        we might laugh
        at the passengers
        in that bus.
              But aren't we also
              cutting up our community
              all the time
              in parts and parcels,

in groups and classes,
in peoples and tribes?
It is undivine,
it is unchristian,
it is stupid.
Jesus admits
that there are different
functions:
there are lawyers and workers,
there are men and women,
there are scribes and their disciples,
but we all are
CHILDREN OF GOD,
brothers and sisters,
who should serve each other.
And the more talents
you have,
the more you should
serve,
and the more you serve,
the greater you will be
according to the standards
of
Jesus Christ.

51.

A KINGDOM NOW

Matthew 25:1-13

That a bride is late
is quite common
over here in this chapel.
In fact the bride is practically
always late.
It might vary from ten minutes
to three hours,
but late she is.
> It is rare that the bridegroom
> is late.
> He is mostly on time,
> and he is always
> the person most worried
> about the lateness of his bride.
He usually waits here
in the chapel,
nervous,
with his flower falling
from his buttonhole,
consulting his best man,
sending messengers,
and sitting in that first pew
over there,

praying very hard
for a rather obvious
intention:
that she may come
soon.
>But it would be unimaginable
>that *he* would be late,
>so late that it would become
>midnight.
There are other strange things
about the story of the text
of today.
>Where is the bride?
>She is not even mentioned.
>Who are those bridesmaids?
>What does the bridegroom enter?
>How was it possible
>for those bridesmaids,
>the foolish ones,
>to get the advice from
>the wise ones,
>to go and buy oil
>at midnight?
Were there in Jesus' time
already local petrol stations
open twenty-four hours a day?
>This strange story
>is almost always used
>to warn us
>that we should be ready
>to die
>at any moment
>of the day.
That is, indeed,
a very wholesome thought,
and a very necessary one, too,
in our day and age,
but, nevertheless,

it does not seem
    the gist,
    the point,
    or the message of the
    story,
because it would not be
in the line of Jesus
to suggest
that the kingdom of heaven
    —and that is what the story
    is about—
comes to us only
at the end of our lives.
It might come
in its fulfilment
at the end of our lives,
but that fulfilment
will come only
insofar as we stayed awake
in view of it
during our lives over here.
That seems to be the message
of this parable:
that we,
during our lives over here,
should not fall asleep,
but we should keep awake
and ready
at any time that Jesus
wants to invade
our lives
with his kingdom.
    You know what that kingdom is,
    you know what heaven
    is supposed to be.
    You can describe it in different ways.
    For a hungry person
    it is food.

For a thirsty person
it is drink.
For a homeless person
it is home.
For a learned person
it is knowledge.
For a blind person
it is light.
For a deaf person
it is music.
For a lonely person
it is communication.
It is always
a total fulfilment
of our human capacities,
    psychologically,
    physically,
    spiritually,
    and humanly.
The kingdom of God
is human life to the full:
the type of life
that appeared in Jesus.
    Boris Pasternak
    said this beautifully
    in his book *Dr. Zhivago:*
        "and then in this tasteless heap
        of gold and marble,
        HE came,
        light and clothed in an aura
        emphatically human,
        deliberately provincial,
        Galilean,
        and at that moment
        Gods and nations
        ceased to be,
        and
        MAN CAME INTO BEING."

It is that type of fullness
he wants to introduce
into our lives,
not only at the end of them
but now:
humankind being the bride,
he being the bridegroom,
and the kingdom
on the way.

52.

LET US NOT BE AFRAID

Matthew 25:14-30

The Gospel of today
is a Gospel at the end of the
liturgical year.
It is a typical
"last Sundays of the year"
Gospel.
It is about the final account
to be rendered;
about the final examination
to be passed,
about the ultimate
graduation.
>There are those who did well.
>They are praised.
>There are those who did not do
>so well,
>in fact there is that one
>who did not do
>anything at all,
>and his fate is rather
>horrible.
All this is not new.
It is all well known.

Maybe it is even one of those
teachings best known
of all.
>That is why
>it is maybe not the most useful thing
>to give
>another threatening picture of hell;
>it might be better
>to dig a bit deeper
>into this story
>to see what really happened
>to that man
>who fell short
>during his life
>here on earth.
Why did he not move?
Why did he remain fruitless?
Why did he bury his talent?
Why did he remain undeveloped?
>The reason is given:
>he did not move
>because he was afraid;
>it is that fear that made him
>motionless.
>It is fear that did him
>in.
>It is fear that made him not use
>his talent.
>It is fear that made him not love
>as he should have done.
Fear is terrible,
fear is hopeless,
fear is loveless.
>Very, very long ago,
>the Jews had left Egypt.
>They left it in very strange circumstances.
>All the elements in nature,
>>water,
>>fire,

> light,
> insects,
> the sea,
> and so on,
> had worked miraculously
> with them.
> God himself had backed them up,
> and they had marched up to the
> border
> of the *promised land*.

When they arrived there,
Moses stopped his people.
Twelve spies were chosen
to inspect the new land,
one out of each tribe.
They left;
they penetrated the new land
in disguise.
After forty days
they returned.
They brought two reports
with them.
There was a majority report
and there was a minority report.
The minority report
was from two spies only,
Joshua and Caleb.
It read:

> The land is beautiful,
> the land is plenty,
> the land is unbelievable,
> we are going to make it.
> God brought us up to here,
> God is going to bring us there.
> His will be done,
> if we only do not lose
> hope,
> hope being
> a passion for the possible.

But this prophetic minority
was overshadowed
by the other ten,
the majority.
They counselled prudence.
They were practical, they said.
They were realistic, they said.
Their report read:
> The land through which we went
> to collect information
> is terrific,
> but so are its inhabitants.
> They are so big,
> that we seemed like grasshoppers
> to them,
> but to ourselves as well.
> We are never going to make it.
> The obstacles are too great.
> Let us go back home.

At that,
according to the available information,
the whole people
raised a loud cry
and they took stones
to kill Joshua and Caleb,
and they shouted:
"Away with those two,
away with Moses,
let us choose ourselves
another leader,
let us go back
to Egypt."
> They were afraid
> and ready to forget
> all that had happened.
> They were afraid,
> and ready to bury
> all that God had done to them
> in the desert sand.

But then God interfered;
the earth split open
and the ten prophets of doom
were buried by God,
and a voice was heard
telling them
that they would have to wait
for another forty years
before they would be allowed
to enter
the promised land.
>It was their fear that undid them,
>just as it was fear
>that frustrated
>the man with the one talent.
The times of a promised land
are over,
but the time of a promised time,
not at all.
The whole of the Bible
is looking for a new stage
in human history,
for a time
in which there will be
justice and equality
for all,
a time in which everyone
can grow out
to fullness,
>a new time
>about which one is
>thinking so much
>at this moment
>in this world,
>a time free of corruption,
>a time free of misery,
>a time without lost children.
But now too
we seem to be divided:

there is that minority
that believes in it;
there is that minority
that works at it.
      There is also a majority
      that says:
            It will never come about;
            things will not get better;
            they can only get worse;
            there is at the moment even
            more corruption
            than ever before.
            Nothing will change.
            The powerful ones are too big,
            and we are too small,
            insects only.
            The obstacles are too
            formidable.
            The economic powers
            too forceful.
            If we resist them
            we are going to be squashed.
So let us accommodate,
let us be practical,
let us be realistic,
let us be on the safe side;
      and all hope goes,
      and all prophecy stops,
      and nothing
      ever
      would happen
      if that majority
      were listened to;
      and the Joshua
      and Caleb
      of our days
      are going to be stoned
      to death.

That is what the story of today
is about.
It is about the fear
of that man
who, instead of pressing forward,
held back
and forgot
that God is even more ahead of us
than above us.
>   That is what we Christians
>   forget too often.
>   We should be of the prophetic
>   minority,
>   not afraid
>   of bringing out the good
>   in us
>   and others,
>   pushing forward,
>   to a world,
>   to better times
>   to come.

53.

JESUS CHRIST KING

Matthew 25:31-46

Something strange seems to overcome
Jesus,
  that man,
  who always had been serving others;
  that man,
  who had run away when they wanted
  to make him king;
  that man,
  who had washed the feet
  of his disciples;
  that man,
  who had called a child the most important
  issue in the world
  and not himself;
  that man,
  who had told his disciples not to rule,
  not to master over others;
  that man
  calls himself in one of his last speeches,
  according to Saint Matthew,
  at least twice
  KING.

Very many people say
that the time of kings is over,
and that is true
now.
But in the Old Testament
that was not true
at all.
    The word "king"
    is one of the more frequently used
    words.
    The word "king"
    is used over 2,500
    times in the Old Testament.
One expected in that time
very much from a king.
Those expectations
were often expressed.
In Psalm 72
one prays for the king:
    "Give to the king
    YOUR JUDGMENT,
    O God,
    and to his son
    YOUR JUSTICE.
    Let him guide your people
    justly.
    Let him help the poor
    with dignity;
        in that way
        the mountains
        will carry peace
        and the hills
        justice.
    Let him understand
    the plight of the poor,
    let him assist
    their children,

let him do away
with oppression."
That is what
one expected
from a king,
and it was
definitely
in that line of thought
that Christ
called himself
KING.
Think of that day
in Nazareth
when he took
the Old Testament
to explain himself,
and how he rolled that scroll
down
to this passage
in Isaiah:
The SPIRIT of God
is upon me
—that is what one had prayed for
in Psalm 72—
he has anointed me
to assist the poor,
—again an echo from that
psalm—
to heal the contrite,
to liberate prisoners,
to help those in trouble.
So king he was
and yet,
when we take
the reading of today
something like a transfer
takes place,

because in the description
of that final judgment
WE, humankind,
do not come together
to judge
whether *he*
has been a good
king.
HE
is judging *us,*
on those very same issues.
He, the king,
is judging
us
in how far we have been
KING.
He turns
the roles
around
completely
and says:
    "What did YOU do,
    when you saw
    anybody
    hungry
    or
    thirsty
    or
    oppressed
    or
    in need
    or
    in prison."
In that change of roles
he even goes so far
that he,
THE KING,

identifies
with those poor.
  Brothers and sisters,
  at this feast of
  JESUS CHRIST KING,
  on the last Sunday
  of the liturgical year,
  we are supposed
  to understand
  that it is up to us,
  to all of us,
  to rule as the kings
  in the Old Testament
  were supposed
  to rule.
  It is not in vain
  that we,
  all of us,
  were anointed
  priest, prophet, and KING
  at our baptism.
Those kings were supposed
to be life-
and hope-giving.
They were supposed
to make others
grow;
they were supposed
to widen their hearts and minds;
they were supposed
to liberate and save,
to open and develop.
  Brothers and sisters,
  do you live like a king,
  do you live like a queen,
  does justice roll
  from you

over the mountains
and over the hills,
over the whole of the
land?
Because
that is the question
he is going to ask
you
in the end:
Have you ever
been like
HIM,
our KING?
Amen, amen.

INDEX OF SCRIPTURAL TEXTS

Matthew

1:18-25	23
2:1-12	38
2:13-15, 19-23	34
3:1-12	11
4:1-11	67
4:12-23	48
5:1-12	54
5:13-16	60
7:21-27	155
9:9-13	161
9:36-10:8	168
10:26-33	175
11:2-11	17
11:25-30	186
13:1-23	194
13:24-43	200
13:44-52	205
14:13-21	213
14:22-33	228
16:13-20	234
16:21-27	239
17:1-9	74
18:15-20	244
18:21-35	248
20:1-16	252
21:28-32	255
21:33-43	259
22:1-14	264
22:15-21	271
22:34-40	277
23:1-12	283
24:37-44	1
25:1-13	288
25:14-30	293
25:31-46	300
26:14-27:36	95
26:19-20	113

John

1:29-34	42
3:16-18	146
4:5-42	79
6:51-58	149
9:1-41	87
10:1-10	114
11:1-45	91
14:1-12	119
14:15-21	126
20:1-9	99
20:19-23	140
20:19-31	104
21:15-19	181

Luke

2:1-14	28
24:13-35	108

Other Orbis Titles

GOD, WHERE ARE YOU?

by Carlos Mesters

Meditations and reflections on significant figures and events in the Bible. "We shall," says Mesters, "try to restore to the word of God the function that it ought to have: to serve as a light on the pathway of life, as a help to our own understanding of present-day reality in all its complexity."

ISBN 0-88344-162-4 CIP   *Cloth $6.95*

THE EXPERIENCE OF GOD

by Charles Magsam

"His range is comprehensive; his orientation is personal, biblical, communitarian; his tone is positive and encouraging: all in all, a one-volume course on how to be free wholesomely for God, for oneself and for others." *Prairie Messenger*

ISBN 0-88344-123-3   *Cloth $7.95*

ISBN 0-88344-124-1   *Paper $4.95*

JESUS OF NAZARETH

Meditations on His Humanity

by Jose Comblin

"St. Teresa of Avila warned her nuns to beware of any kind of prayer that would seek to eliminate all reference to the human aspect of Christ. I think Jose Comblin would agree that her warning also describes the theme of his extremely valuable book that can be read and re-read many times with great benefit." *Priests USA*

ISBN 0-88344-231-0   *Cloth $5.95*

PRAYER AT THE HEART OF LIFE

by Brother Pierre-Yves Emery

"Emery's approach is both realistic and down-to-earth and profound and moving. This book can be recommended to anyone interested in a practical analysis of prayer, particularly the specific relationship between prayer and life itself." *Review for Religious*

ISBN 0-88344-393-7   *Cloth $4.95*

PILGRIMAGE TO NOW/HERE

by Frederick Franck

"Every now and then a true gem of a book appears that fails to get caught up in the tide of promotion, reviews, and sales, and, despite its considerable merits, seems to disappear. Such a book is Dr. Frederick Franck's *Pilgrimage to Now/Here*. His *Zen of Seeing* has been a steady seller, and *The Book of Angelus Silesius* is moving well. What happened to *Pilgrimage*, which in many ways is a more important book? Since Orbis is known as a religious publishing house, many distributors and booksellers are reluctant to stock it. Yet this is a religious book in the most significant sense of that word—in what Frederick Franck would call the search for meaning—for it is an account of a modern pilgrimage by jet, bus, train, and on foot to visit holy places and meet Buddhist leaders and Zen masters in India, Ceylon, Hong Kong and Japan."

East West Journal
ISBN 0-88344-387-2   *Illustrated Paper $3.95*

BIBLICAL REVELATION AND AFRICAN BELIEFS

edited by Kwesi Dickson and Paul Ellingworth

"Essays by scholars who are themselves both African and Christian and who share a concern that Christian theology and African thought be related to each other in a responsible and creative way. There is no comparable book; this one should be in any library attempting serious coverage of either African thought or Christian theology." *Choice*

ISBN 0-88344-033-4   *Cloth $5.95*
ISBN 0-88344-034-2   *Paper $3.45*

IN SEARCH OF THE BEYOND
by Carlo Carretto

"The book describes an 'aloneness' that draws hearts closer together, a 'withdrawal' that enriches family and community ties, a love of God that deepens human love." *America*

ISBN 0-88344-208-6   *Cloth $5.95*

LETTERS FROM THE DESERT
by Carlo Carretto

"It has been translated into Spanish, French, German, Portuguese, Arabic, Japanese, Czech, and now, gracefully enough (from Italian) into English. I hope it goes into twenty-four more editions. It breathes with life, with fresh insights, with wisdom, with love." *The Thomist*

ISBN 0-88344-279-5   *Cloth $4.95*

THE GOD WHO COMES
by Carlo Carretto

"This is a meaty book which supplies on every page matter for reflection and a spur to the laggard or wayward spirit. It offers true Christian perspective." *Our Sunday Visitor*

ISBN 0-88344-164-0   *Cloth $4.95*

FREEDOM TO BE FREE
By Arturo Paoli

"Full of eye-opening reflections on how Jesus liberated man through poverty, the Cross, the Eucharist and prayer." *America*

ISBN 0-88344-143-8   *Paper $4.95*

SILENT PILGRIMAGE TO GOD
The Spirituality of Charles de Foucauld

by a Little Brother of Jesus
preface by Rene Voillaume

"Sets out the main lines of Charles de Foucauld's spirituality and offers selections from his writings." *America*

ISBN 0-88344-459-3   *Cloth $4.95*

AFRICAN TRADITIONAL RELIGION: A DEFINITION

by E. Bolaji Idowu

"This important book is the first to place the study of African religion in the larger context of religious studies. . . . It includes an index and notes. There is no comparable work; this one should be in any collection on African religion." *Choice*

ISBN 0-88344-005-9   *Cloth $6.95*

THE PATRIOT'S BIBLE

edited by John Eagleson and Philip Scharper

"Following the terms of the Declaration of Independence and the U.S. Constitution, this faithful paperback relates quotes from the Bible and from past and present Americans 'to advance the kingdom and further our unfinished revolution.' " *A.D.*

ISBN 0-88344-377-5   *Paper $3.95*

THE RADICAL BIBLE

adapted by John Eagleson and Philip Scharper

"I know no book of meditations I could recommend with more confidence to learned and unlearned alike." *St. Anthony Messenger*

ISBN 0-88344-425-9   *Cloth $3.95*
ISBN 0-88344-426-7   *Pocketsize, paper $1.95*

UGANDA: THE ASIAN EXILES

by Thomas and Margaret B. Melady

"Takes its inspiration from the announcement in August 1972 by General Idi Amin Dada, President of Uganda, that he was told in a dream to order the expulsion of all Asians from Uganda. Tom and Margaret Melady were there and were witness to the tragic events. The book surveys the gruesome events following the expulsion order and the irrational pattern of Amin's record as well as providing a factual background of the Asian presence in Africa. The historical, economic and social complexity of the African-Asian-European situation in Uganda is made clear. Stories of personal devotion and heroism put flesh on the facts." *Religious Media Today*

ISBN 0-88344-506-9 CIP   *Cloth $6.95*